ARTHUR RANSOME

and the world of the Swallows and Amazons

Roger Wardale

GREAT NORTHERN

Published by Great Northern Books,
Holebottom Farm, Hebden, Skipton, North Yorkshire, BD23 5DL.

Copyright © Roger Wardale and Great Northern Books 2000

ISBN: 0 9535035 4 2

Design and layout: Trevor Ridley
Printed by The Amadeus Press Ltd, West Yorkshire

British Cataloguing in Publication Data
A catalogue record for this book is available from the British Library

CONTENTS

Arthur Ransome

INTRODUCING ARTHUR RANSOME

The story of four children who borrow a sailing dinghy and camp on an island in the Lake District, where they meet a couple of high-spirited local girls and the hostile stranger they call Captain Flint, was to change not only 'the course of children's literature', as one critic put it, but also the life of its author, Arthur Ransome.

Yet *Swallows and Amazons* was not an immediate best-seller, in spite of some good reviews, mostly written by his friends, when it entered the world of children's fiction in the summer of 1930. Its author was better known to readers of the *Manchester Guardian* for his fishing essays, and was perhaps remembered by a few for his first-hand reports of the Russian Revolution in 1917. Arthur Ransome was 46 years old and had turned down the promise of a steady £1,000-a-year job with the *Guardian* expressly to make one final attempt at writing fiction. In his precarious venture he had the support of his second wife, Evgenia, whom he had rescued from St Petersburg and brought home to England in 1925.

A chance meeting with the publisher Jonathan Cape had elicited an invitation for Ransome to collect together some of his fishing essays to be published as an anthology. When instead he nervously presented a brief outline and a list of chapter headings for his children's story, Cape casually offered him a contract and agreed to pay an advance of £100 with the guarded proviso '...it's the essays we want.'

Not only did Ransome's publisher find the title 'Swallows and Amazons' somewhat dull, he soon discovered the irascible side of his budding new author who summarily dismissed the drawings that had been commissioned to illustrate the story. Yet in spite of such an inauspicious start, in the 70 years since its first publication, the book has remained continuously in print, with a sale to date of more than 300,000 hardback copies and many more in paperback editions. The story has been made into a feature film, and it now ranks as a modern classic among children's literature. Twelve more Swallows stories were to follow, the last discovered unfinished among Ransome's papers after his death and published in 1988 in a collection entitled *Coots in the North*.

Until the publication of Ransome's letters, *Signalling from Mars*, in 1997, few of the admirers, who had swelled his worldwide sales in many languages to some five million copies, guessed what it cost him to produce the books. Working in the shadow of his wife's unsparing criticism and the ever-present threat of ill-health, Ransome was constantly assailed by self-doubt. 'I am having the most frightful struggle to pull it into shape,' he wrote to his publishers while he wrestled with *Winter Holiday* only weeks before it was due to appear in the bookshops for the Christmas season. Still, of one thing he was sure:

> I believe that no matter who reads it, a good book is always one written by the author for himself. This is true even of the good books whose authors mistakenly supposed that they were writing for children. Alice is a good book not because the story was first invented 'for' a young Miss Liddell, but because Lewis Carroll got a great deal of private fun out of writing it for himself. And you do not suppose that Stevenson wrote *Treasure Island* for anyone but himself.

In an abandoned biography of his favourite childhood author, Ransome confided that Robert

Louis Stevenson's secret depended, 'not on the description of circumstances pleasurable in themselves, but on a tenderness exhibited by the writer for his subject, on the infectious quality of the mood in which a man can look upon his past.'

Of his own past Arthur Ransome once said, 'Mine has not been a life of consistent effort towards a single end. It seems to me that I've been like a shuttlecock, bandied to and fro by lunatics. I seem to have lived not one life, but snatches from a dozen different lives'. It was those various 'lives' which gave Ransome the ingredients for the alchemy that eventually produced the Swallows and Amazons books.

ACKNOWLEDGEMENTS

My first debt is to my publisher David Joy for asking me if I would like to produce one more book about Arthur Ransome, so enabling me to realise a long-standing dream to publish a selection of colour photographs of the places mentioned in the Swallows and Amazons canon. In spite of a having a photographic collection which was started when colour became readily available in the 1960s, almost all the colour photographs reproduced here have been taken specially for this book and have not been seen in print before.

I must thank Arthur Ransome's executors John Bell and Christina Hardyment for generously allowing me once more to plunder the rich store of Ransome material and particularly for permitting me to quote at length from his published and unpublished writings.

Tony Colwell, formally my editor at Jonathan Cape, has been invaluable in shaping the text and helping me with the difficult task of revisiting a subject about which I have said so much already. The result is a text which does not merely support the photographs, but has a strong biographical element and provides an insight into the trials and tribulations which lay behind the seemingly effortless prose of the Swallows and Amazons books. At the same time, I have tried to address the question that generations of young readers have asked — 'Is it true?'.

Ted Alexander has also been immensely helpful and allowed me to make use of his own extensive collection of photographs, and I have also been able to call upon his considerable knowledge of Ransome's time spent in Eastern Europe.

Everyone writing about Ransome since 1984 has been able to build on the foundations laid by Hugh Brogan and Christina Hardyment. More recently Hugh Brogan's collection of selected letters, Signalling From Mars has complemented his earlier biography.

The bulk of Ransome's papers are among the Special Collections at the Brotherton Library at the University of Leeds. I would like to thank Christopher Sheppard for permission to reproduce images from the collection, and his staff, notably Ann Farr, for their helpfulness during my visits.

The Ransome Room at Abbot Hall Museum of Lakeland Life and Industry has fascinated enthusiasts for some years, but less well known has been their collection of hundreds of sketches made by Ransome as a basis for his illustrations. These have now been photographed and the entire collection is now readily available for study. My selection, Ransome the Artist was produced in collaboration with Abbot Hall in 1998 and is available from the museum, and I thank the Director, Edward King, for allowing me to reproduce images from that book.

My thanks to Windermere Steamboat Museum for allowing me to reproduce my photographs of Esperance, one of the floating exhibits in their unique collection.

I am grateful to Lydia Spurrier for giving me permission to reproduce her late father's wonderful map for Swallows and Amazons and to Blakes Holidays Ltd for the pages from their 1947 edition of Norfolk Broads Holidays Afloat.

Random House have allowed me to reproduce photographs from their collection and to include a number of extracts from the Jonathan Cape archive at the University of Reading which contains correspondence between Ransome and Jonathan Cape's partner G. Wren Howard.

I would also like to thank the following for their help: David Alcock, David Allcock, Taqui Altounyan, Gillian Beevor, Paul Crisp, the late Mavis Guzelian, David Hutchinson, David Jones, Rebecca Knights, Malcolm Morrison, Ian and Shirley Parker, David Parker, Josephine Russell, David and Elizabeth Sewart, Mike Sparkes. Larissa Thompson and Hazel Vale.

All attempts have been made to identify the rightful copyright holders and if anyone has been missed out through lack of information, we express our sincere apologies.

Chapter One

YOUTHFUL AMBITION

The entry in Arthur Ransome's diary for 24th March 1929 says simply, 'Started S & A.' That day, in an old bank barn which had been turned into a workroom, he had written the opening four pages of text. The room was large enough to allow him to pace about when writing became difficult. The actual writing took place at a large table — or rather two tables placed together and covered with a blanket, beside which stood an ominously large wastepaper basket. Ransome liked to write, surrounded by mementos from his travels, such as his pocket compass bought in Reval in Estonia, a lucky stone from the summit of Coniston Old Man, a tiny telescope and a carved figure of an Egyptian cat. His wife Evgenia dismissed them as 'Arthur's toys', but their presence gave welcome support. Two good-sized windows with seats faced south across the valley. A comfortable 'literary' chair in which he did his reading, some bookcases and a stuffed fish on the wall completed the furnishing.

The barn still stands beside the cottage in the Lake District to which Ransome brought his Russian wife in 1925. Their home — Low Ludderburn — was tiny; just two up and two down with a lean-to addition. Two acres of woodland, fruit trees and garden adjoined the cottage which stands high above the Winster Valley not far from Lake Windermere. Down on the lake his newly acquired sailing dinghy *Swallow* swung on her moorings, and the previous day he had sailed with Evgenia to the lakeside Storrs Hall Hotel for tea, and then drifted home in the evening.

In one of his accounts of the origin of *Swallows and Amazons*, Ransome said that it came to him during his first real sail in *Swallow*. How much of the story was actually planned when they sailed slowly home in the twilight we shall never know for, as he explained in a note added in 1958, it had its beginning forty years earlier when his father, Cyril Ransome, took his wife and children for their summer holidays to the hamlet of High Nibthwaite near the foot of Coniston Water in the Lake District. The farm where they stayed, the woods, the beck, the tarn and lakeside became the children's playground, and the animals and the local people were their friends. Young Arthur was enchanted, and throughout his life he returned again and again in reality and in imagination. As soon as they arrived, he would run joyfully down to the lake shore, plunge his hands into the water and wish. A note in the typescript of *Swallows and Amazons* says, 'If I were to dip and wish today, my wish would be that people meeting those children for the first time should enjoy reading their book as much as I enjoyed watching it grow.'

Cyril Ransome and his young wife had been married for two years when in 1884 the first of their four children was born. Arthur Michell was followed by sisters, Cecily and Joyce, and a brother, Geoffrey. After a successful academic career at Oxford and some tutoring at Rugby, their father had taken up a post as Professor of Modern History at Yorkshire College (now the University of Leeds). The family lived close to the College and their children were brought up in a solid middle-class academic world.

The Ransomes were descended from East Anglian millers, though Arthur's great-grandfather practised as a surgeon and was one of the founders of the Manchester Medical School. His grandfather was a gifted, but feckless scientist-inventor who flitted from one unproductive scheme to another.

Cyril, on the other hand, had developed an interest in politics and was a regular speaker on the Liberal platform. He wrote several history and English books and the additional income from these had enabled him to pay off his father's mounting debts. His wife, Edith Boulton, came from a wealthy Anglo-Australian family. Edward Baker Boulton had emigrated to Australia, bought vast areas of land where he farmed sheep, had married and returned to England with a family of seven young children. Shortly after his arrival his wife died and he quickly remarried, raising a second family of ten, of whom Edith was the eldest.

In their different ways, both grandfathers influenced the young Arthur. Grandfather Boulton was much more interested in painting than he was in sheep. He is still remembered in Australia as an accomplished artist whose work commands good prices. Even more interesting than watching his grandfather paint were visits they made to Bristol Docks which Arthur had read about in *Treasure Island*. Grandmother Emma was the first of several formidable women in Ransome's life, and from her the child learnt the moves of chess — a game which was to become a lifelong source of pleasure. Grandfather Ransome was an excellent field-naturalist and by taking his grandson on country walks, he laid the foundation for Arthur's lasting interest in natural history. The boy kept an aquarium, and when the summer holidays were over and the time came for a tearful return to Leeds, his newly acquired collection of caterpillars and minnows went with him

Rearing caterpillars and keeping white rats were among the few pleasures of Arthur's life at the Old College, Windermere, where he was as miserable as only a misfit at boarding school can be. He had learnt to read at a very early age, almost certainly having been taught by his mother. At first his education had begun at home with Ric Eddison, the son of one of his father's friends. Secure in their mutual support, the two naughty little boys made life as difficult as possible for a string of inexperienced tutors. Next followed a short period when Arthur attended a nearby day school where he was happy and had a 'kind, intelligent' teacher. At the age of eight, he wrote a story about a desert island in a tiny red notebook. In the story two boys are wrecked on the island:

They built a house and a stockade round it to keep it safe from wild beasts or savages if any should come. Tom shot a wild duck and a sort of pigeon which lasted for breakfast and dinner and they found some bananas and coconuts for tea. There was a little stream running through underneath the stockade so that they should never run short of water. Jack nevertheless took two or three barrels and filled them with water in case the stream dried up. They also gathered a great deal of fruit to preserve because if they were attacked by savages they would not be able to get out to get any.

The following year, Arthur had the misfortune to transfer from a day school whose ethos encouraged the love of learning to one where boys were not expected learn, except under duress. Unlike his first school, the Old College gave undue prestige to those who excelled at boxing and organised games. Poor sight made Arthur a muff at games and he found himself ridiculed by the other boys, none of whom came from a similar academic background. The only relief came on Sundays when it was possible to escape for a few hours to visit Great Aunt Susan who lived up by Windermere Station. Help was not to be had where he might have expected to find it, for the staff, apart from the headmaster's wife, were largely unsympathetic. Once, he tried to draw attention to his plight by running away, but the school authorities were careful to hush up the affair and his parents were never told.

Unfortunately Cyril Ransome thought he saw in his eldest son the very weakness he regretted in his own father. He did not recognise Arthur's sudden enthusiasms and his inability to sustain any activity for long as a stage through which many boys pass. Confronted by a continual negative attitude, time and time again Arthur felt that he had failed his father. Familiar and successful as the Professor may have been with young adults, he showed little imagination and understanding of his eldest child. He subjected the boy to some bizarre experiments, such as being tossed overboard from a boat on Coniston Water to see if he could swim, and expecting him, when very young, to learn three languages simultaneously. What Cyril Ransome *did* share with his son was a deep love for the Lake District and, as the boy grew older, an enthusiasm for fishing.

When the time came to look ahead to the next school, Cyril Ransome resigned from the Yorkshire College and the family moved to Rugby where it was anticipated a little sixth form tutoring and the income from his books would keep the family going until he could enter Parliament. However, his injury in a fishing accident some years earlier eventually cost him his life when the leg turned tubercular. Cyril Ransome died at the age of 46, just after Arthur had failed miserably in the Rugby scholarship examination.

Arthur entered Rugby without a scholarship, and at the school formed several important friendships, notably with Ted Scott, whose father was editor of the *Manchester Guardian* for 57 years. The two boys once completed an eleven-mile cross-country run, not in a race, but purely for their own satisfaction. Yet some boys are always ready to make life unpleasant for those who are a little unusual, and Arthur continued to suffer from bullying. By good fortune, however, he came under the influence of a great classical scholar, W.H.D. Rouse, who discovered his secret ambition to become a writer. In doing everything he could to encourage and help the boy, Dr Rouse dismayed Arthur's mother. Mrs Ransome regarded writing as anything but the sort of safe career towards which she wanted to steer her son. Eventually she became one of his staunchest supporters and her good opinion of a book was much valued.

After matriculating, Ransome returned to Leeds where he dutifully read science for a couple of terms at Yorkshire College. The call to leave science for ever and make writing his career became irresistible when he read of William Morris and the art and craft movement which had rebelled against the increasing mechanisation of industry by creating beautiful things. Ransome absorbed the ideals of the movement and in later years would rail against what he considered inferior books by calling them 'machine made'. Even at college, where he took to reading William Hazlett's essays instead of scientific textbooks, Ransome never lost his attachment to fairy stories. Almost overnight he decided that what he really wanted to do was to write stories for children and

Arthur Ransome at Rugby from a group photo of his house fifteen taken around 1901.

become an essayist like Hazlett.

He persuaded his mother to allow him to abandon college and take a job in London as a publisher's errand boy with Grant Richards. Shortly afterwards Mrs Ransome left Rugby and moved to Balham in south London, taking her family with her. Weary of working long hours that gave him no time for writing, Ransome moved to the struggling Unicorn Press. As soon as he had earned a holiday, he took off for Coniston in the summer of 1903 and there, quite by chance, met the man who, above all others, was to support and encourage him in his chosen career. At the time of their meeting Ransome was lying on a rock in the middle of the Coppermines Beck, which flows from Coppermines Valley down to Coniston village, struggling to write poetry, while an artist was returning home after painting somewhere up on the Old Man. The painter wondered whether the body on the rock was dead and called out, 'Are you alive, young man?'

*Arthur Ransome arriving in Bohemia on the tailboard of a van. One of Fred Taylor's illustrations for **Bohemia in London.***

The young man was very much alive and explained what he was doing to the highly talented W.G. Collingwood, the writer and Norse scholar who had been Ruskin's amanuensis and biographer. Something about Ransome must have appealed to Collingwood, for he invited him to call at his home, Lanehead, on the opposite side of the lake. Just before his holiday ended Ransome followed up the invitation and was made welcome by Collingwood and his equally talented wife who painted portrait miniatures. They told him to come again next time he was in the area.

When Ransome returned to London, he set about acquiring lodgings and found himself a flat in the artists' quarter of Chelsea. He told the story of the move a year or so later in *Bohemia in London*:

At last I spent a morning prowling round Chelsea, and found an empty room with four windows all in

good condition, and a water supply two floors below at a rent of a few shillings a week. I paid for a week in advance and went home ordering a grocer's van to call. After lunch the van drew up before the door. I announced it's meaning, packed all my books into it, a railway rug, a bundle of clothes and my one large chair, said good-bye to my relations, and then, after lighting my clay pipe, and seating myself complacently on the tailboard, gave the order to start. I was as Columbus setting forth to a New World, a gypsy striking his tent for unknown woods; I felt as if I had been a wanderer in a caravan from my childhood as I loosened my coat, opened one or two more buttons on my flannel shirt that I wore open at the neck, and saw the red brick houses slipping slowly away behind me. The pride of it, to be sitting behind a van that I had hired myself; to carry my own belongings to a place of my own choosing; to be absolutely a free man, whose most distant desires seemed instantly attainable. I have never known another afternoon like that.

Ransome was not yet twenty. He managed to scrape a living from reviews, essays and by undertaking some hack work. The first book to bear his name was the unlikely *A.B.C. of Physical Culture*. In the book he adopts the tone of a sage, and pontificates on such matters as the benefits of swimming, and the dangers of drinking too much fluid. At this time he was reading voraciously and used to say that for him London was marked by bookshops as the sea was by buoys.

The following summer, with a little money in his pocket and a little work to keep him going, Ransome headed north once more to Coniston and the Collingwoods. After a few days in the village he was invited to stay at Lanehead as the two younger children were away at school. Mrs Collingwood became Ransome's 'aunt', and she made him feel part of the family by sending him on errands and allowing him to help with the chores. Her elder children, Dora (18) and Barbara (17), were studying at home, and it would have been surprising if Arthur had not fallen in love. Those weeks were among the happiest of his life. He joined the girls when they went out painting or took a picnic basket on the lake. After dinner the three talked long into the evening in the 'lair' in the Lanehead garden. Eventually it was time for

Robin and Ursula to return home and Mrs Collingwood helped Ransome to pack. His things were in the 'most hopeless confusion', Dora noted. 'I have made a bet with him, a cob pipe against a 2d indiarubber that he will come back next year'. She had also spotted that 'something was going on' between Arthur and Barbara. 'She pretends not to care in the least, but I have my doubts!'

Peggoty Cole, an artist friend of Ransome's, was also quick to notice that he had fallen in love, although she thought it 'much too early'. In the autumn, Dora and Barbara were due to enrol at Cope's Drawing Studio, and Peggoty helped Ransome to find lodgings for Mrs Collingwood and the girls barely two minutes from his own in Chelsea. The girls saw a lot of Ransome that winter, calling at his lodgings and listening appreciatively to his latest piece of writing. Towards the end of October Ransome proposed to Barbara. When she refused him, he took himself off to Surrey, until a letter from Mrs Collingwood brought him back home. After his return, life seems to have continued much as before.

The Collingwoods had made it clear that Ransome would be welcome at Lanehead the following summer, but he decided to stay elsewhere. The poet Gordon Bottomley found him lodgings

Lanehead, the home of the Collingwood family, was owned by Miss Emma Holt of the Liverpool shipping line who allowed them to live there rent-free. Nowadays it is used as an Outdoor Education Centre by Cleveland Education Committee.

at Wall Nook, a farmhouse near Cartmel, where, from time to time, he set out to walk to Lanehead to visit Barbara, whom he still hoped to marry. It was a walk not to be undertaken lightly, for it involved a round trip of more than thirty miles, usually completed in the dark.

While Ransome was at Wall Nook he wrote three little nature books for children in which he, in the person of the Ogre, earnestly instructs the Imp and the Elf in the delights of nature study, even managing to enthuse over the habits of slugs and worms. In the final chapter of the third book, *Pond and Stream* the tone changes and Ransome — no doubt recalling picnics on Peel Island with the Collingwood girls — describes a day spent on the lake:

We run the boat out of the boathouse, and when we have settled down, the Elf and the baskets in the stern, and the Imp lying flat on his stomach in the

Dora Collingwood

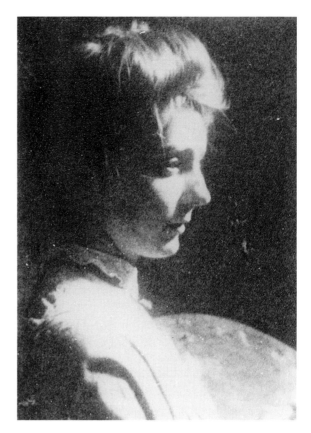

Barbara Collingwood

bows, we slip away down the lake rippling the smooth waters, and leaving long wavelets behind us that make the hills and trees dance in their reflections... of course we are pirates and Sir Francis Drakes, and Vikings and other sea rovers from time to time..

The voyage continues:

We row down the lake, lazily and slowly, past rocky bays and sharp-nosed promontories, and low points pinnacled with firs. The hills change as we row. At the head of the lake they are rugged and high, with black crags on them far away, but lower down the lake they are not so rough. There are fewer rocks and more heather, and the hills are gentler and more mountainous, until at last at the foot of the lake they open into a broad flat valley where the river runs into the sea. A little more than half way down there is an island that we can see, a green dot in the distance from our farmhouse windows, and here we have our

tea... As soon as tea is over we prowl over the rockiness of the little island, and creep among the hazels and pines and tiny oaks and undergrowth. Do you know trees never look so beautiful as when you get peeps of water between their fluttering leaves? When we have picked our way through to the other end, we climb upon a high rock with a flat top to it, and heather growing in its crevices; and here we lie, torpid after our tea and pretend we are Viking-folk from the north who have forced our way here by land and sea, and are looking for the first time upon a lake that no one knew before us.

It would be a quarter of a century before Ransome returned in fiction to the lake country and a similar voyage of discovery.

The following year Ransome persuaded his own family to stay for a month at How Head, a short distance up the road from Lanehead, so that he could drop in on the Collingwoods just when it suited him, often staying for hours on end, watching the girls at work — so far as work was possible in the circumstances. Dora thought that Arthur was as much in love with her sister as ever, but she was unable to make out Barbara's feelings. Ransome's name frequently crops up in Dora's journal at this time:

> Last night he walked to Ambleside to meet Pater and Mother and walked back with them — clean forgetting to tell his mother where he was going — and she expecting him in to supper at 7.30 and he didn't get back till after 10. He is the most thoughtless person in some ways — and within a nice man — we all look on him with feelings of affection and amusement.

Barbara Collingwood and Ransome were to remain friends throughout their lives, and she wrote this brief teasing letter fifty years later on his seventy-second birthday:

> This is just a note of condolence on the sad occasion of your birthday. I hope you are bearing up well and forgetting the weight of years in anticipation of all the octos and nonos who are riotously celebrating their birthday all over the place.
>
> I must say you looked extremely un-elderly when you cornered me the other day on the fifth floor of the Festival Hall. Are you still very angry?

Back in Chelsea, Ransome busied himself with *Highways and Byways in Fairyland*. It is a tiny book, just 12cm x 9 cm with a pictorial cover and highly decorative endpapers, which is dedicated to the mysterious 'Q of S'. The chapter headings tell their own story: The Way to Fairyland, The Mountains of the Gnomes, The Water Palace, The Pixie Woods, The Dancing Ring etc. Not surprisingly, Ransome chooses to sail to Fairyland, arriving to the sound of fairy bells and a troupe of fairy dancers on the shore.

Edwardian bohemia suited Ransome. He felt thoroughly at home among the fellowship of struggling writers and artists who gathered of an evening and felt that anything was possible. Included among his literati friends were the poets John Masefield, Gordon Bottomley, Edward Thomas and Lascelles Abercrombie, to whose daughter, Elizabeth, *Swallowdale* is dedicated. The Japanese artist Yoshio Markino was also a friend and another artist, Pixie Colman Smith, became 'Gypsy' in his next book, *Bohemia in London*. At Pixie's 'evening' in her studio they would roar Ransome's favourite shanty, 'Spanish Ladies', after drinking 'opal hush' (claret and fizzy lemonade). Pixie never tired of telling the Anansi stories she had heard as a child in Jamaica, and Ransome claimed that he learnt more of the art of narrative from listening to those stories than he did from any book. He repeated them in his turn for his friends, and there are those who see the origin of Nancy Blackett in the big fat shiny spider Anansi. The stories were well known to Titty Walker, who remembered the obeah woman, 'with wrinkles deep as ditches', when she was making the wax doll in *Swallowdale*.

Several of Ransome's acquaintances made their appearances in *Bohemia in London*, a largely autobiographical tale, although some of Ransome's own experiences are attributed to others. First published in 1907, and reprinted as recently as 1984 in a paperback edition by the Oxford University Press, it is perhaps the most engaging of Ransome's early works. There is a freshness and naivete about the book which is missing from his later work. One chapter is devoted to a day in the life of an artist:

> A large bare room, with no furniture but a divan or a camp-bed, a couple of chairs, an easel, and a model-stand made of a big box that holds a few coats and hats and coloured silks that do duty in a dozen pictures; a big window slanting up across the roof, with blinds to temper its light; canvasses and old paintings without frames leaning against the walls; the artist, his coat off ready for work, strolling up and down with a cigarette between his lips, looking critically and lovingly at the canvas on the easel, and now and again pulling out his watch: that is a fair picture of a studio at about half-past ten on a workaday morning.
>
> There is a tap on the door.
>
> 'Come in!' and a girl slips into the room, apologises for the thousandth time in her life for being so late, and proceeds to change her clothes for the costume that will make her the subject he wants for his picture, and then taking the chair on the top of the costume box, assumes the pose in which she yesterday began to sit.

In 1908 Ransome spent the summer at Low Yewdale, a couple of miles from Lanehead. That year Dora was the object of his affections and they spent some time together. In her journal Dora recorded that after lunch one day...

> he read me various things that he had written, and then we packed the tea basket and went up past Shepherd's Bridge, and got over the wall and down to the beck and picnicked at a lovely spot... He was very nice, he is so utterly different from any other man I know — indeed he is the only man I know well and in spite of his many eccentricities he is really a dear... I don't wonder that our neighbours talk about us, and AR and I equally don't care.

The piece Ransome read was almost certainly the title story from *The Hoofmarks of the Faun* which opens with a description of Low Yewdale Farm where he was staying: 'Under Raven Crag, in the North Country, there is a grey farm with a huge granary built close under the fell, where the meadows give way to rock and bracken on one side and deep woodland on the other.'

The Hoofmarks of the Faun is a collection of five short stories: the title story dated 1908 (and dedicated to his wife!); 'The Footways of Dream', written in 1911, 'Rolf Sigurdson', dedicated to Dora Collingwood and dated 1904; 'The Little Silver Snakes', dedicated to Barbara Collingwood and dated 1905; and an undated story, 'The Ageing Faun', dedicated to Lascelles Abercrombie. The little book was completed by adding a memoir of an obscure writer, Peter Swainson, whom Ransome had met in Chelsea shortly before his death. The earlier stories had remained unpublished until the collection finally appeared in 1911. Ransome was a prolific writer and throughout his working life had many false starts, half-realised ideas and vague notions for essays and stories which were never completed or if completed, failed to find a publisher.

At the end of August, just before he returned to London, Ransome proposed to Dora, who at the time was making a sketch of him and did not think

Two portrait studies in watercolour by Dora Collingwood. It is tempting to associate these paintings with the occasion when Ransome proposed marriage.

he was serious because he seemed to want to marry anyone and everyone. Dora remained fond of Ransome throughout her life, and later that year, when she and Barbara visited him at his Chelsea flat for tea, the subject of his marriage cropped up again. For his part, Ransome was probably still hoping that Dora would change her mind. Instead, she advised him to pursue the other person he had spoken of at Coniston.

Chapter Two
HOLDING TO RANSOME

It was at this time that Ransome temporarily abandoned the idea of writing publishable stories and became absorbed with the technicalities of writing narrative. He began by editing, translating where necessary, and writing introductions to a series of stories under the title of 'The World's Storytellers'. The series ran to nine volumes which included such writers as Poe, Gautier, Balzac, Scott and Hawthorne, and a group he called 'The Essayists'. *A History of Storytelling*, published in 1909, consists of the introductions from 'The World's Storytellers' and a few additional essays. There is a good deal of name-dropping and an assumption that the reader is as well-read as the author. All this seems far removed from *Swallows and Amazons*, yet it does show a master studying his craft. A few pages are devoted to Daniel Defoe, whose *Robinson Crusoe* Ransome had read at an early age:

> He was in love with verisimilitude, and delighted in facts for their own sakes. 'To read Defoe', wrote Charles Lamb, 'is like hearing evidence in a Court of Justice.' No compliment could have pleased him better... (It is interesting to notice that Defoe, a very early realist, obeyed the spirit of Flaubert's maxim, that the writer should be everywhere invisible in his work, and that his books should, so to speak, tell themselves).

Among the first reviews of *Swallows and Amazons* appears the comment: 'One of the great charms of this book is its extreme reasonableness. Mr

Ransome is as thoughtful of detail as Defoe.' Another way in which Ransome's work echoes Defoe's is the manner in which episodes taken from life or borrowed from other writers, and 'originals' of characters appearing in the Swallows and Amazons books, gain appreciably from the metamorphosis. *Robinson Crusoe* was based on Alexander Selkirk's four years of self-imposed exile on a desert island, but as Ransome wrote of Defoe: 'The figure of Selkirk shrinks away like a faint shadow behind that of Crusoe, whose imaginary

Arthur Ransome in 1908 at the time when he met his first wife.

Ransome camping out in 1912. His tent with 'ears' is similar to the one used by the Amazons in Swallows and Amazons.

adventures his own had suggested, and there can be little doubt in anybody's mind as to which of the two is the more credible.'

With this change of direction, Ransome's work was progressing well while his personal life was going through something of a crisis. After he had finally accepted that neither of the Collingwoods was going to marry him, he says in his *Autobiography* that for a time he made a habit of writing love letters to some acquaintance or imaginary lover – and posting some of them! At the age of 24, he very much wanted to be married. His friends were either married, or would soon be married, and he did not want to be left out. It would be an exaggeration to say that any woman would have done; on the other hand, this was the impression he sometimes gave.

One day a group of art students met at Ransome's flat, bringing with them a Miss Ivy Walker. Shortly after arriving, Ivy announced that 'she was not a barmaid', referring to the impropriety of visiting a strange young man's rooms. To which Ransome, who had been accustomed to entertaining the Collingwood girls, replied along the lines of 'Well, we could solve that by getting married.'

He was soon infatuated by Ivy's amazing imagination. Not only could she fantasise any situation, she enjoyed surrounding the simplest act with secrecy and excitement. She was a very attractive woman, two years older than Ransome and light years more mature, worldly and sophisticated. Ransome was good company, but he was determined to succeed as a man of letters and, despite his hankering, was not yet ready for marriage — as Peggoty Cole had recognised. Nevertheless, in January 1909, they became engaged. Ransome wrote to tell Dora, who thought it was all very sudden, considering what his feelings for her had been so recently.

When meeting Ivy's parents, Ransome was introduced to a family completely different to his own, or the Collingwoods. The Walkers were descended from landed gentry. Mr Walker was a qualified solicitor, although he had never practised. Ivy's mother was partly Portuguese and Ivy was their only child. Her parents had competed for her affections, each constantly trying to score off the other.

Ivy Ransome on the donkey cart that they hired for a holiday in 1912.

The Walker family did not want the marriage: Ivy was already engaged to a cousin, with the wedding dress made and all the arrangements in place when she met Ransome. Grandmother Walker wrote a stiff Victorian entreaty, imploring her not to go ahead with the marriage and reminding her of past mistakes made by other members of the family. In spite of (or perhaps because of) the opposition, after a two-month courtship Arthur and Ivy were married by special licence in a registry office on 13th March. They spent their honeymoon in France, and a church service followed on 1st April. It turned out to be a marriage which might have been made in Hell and was regretted almost at the altar. However, married they were, and they set up home in a pleasant cottage found for them by Edward Thomas, close to where he was living in Hampshire. The cottage is some 800 feet above sea level with views over Petersfield to the South Downs. Here Ransome wrote a critical study of Edgar Allan Poe whom he admired.

The following May they moved to lodgings in Bournemouth, where their daughter Tabitha was born, a few minutes walk from the Walkers' home. The event was to prove a strain for Ransome, and as soon as he was able to arrange it, they left with the child to spend a few weeks with Mrs Ransome,

who was now living in Edinburgh.

Ransome and Mr Walker tolerated one another, but Mrs Walker disapproved of Ransome and gave him a hard time whenever they met. He in turn loathed her, kept out of her way as far as possible and detested her prying visits. Problems with Ivy, with his mother-in-law, with broken nights and the demands of a three-month-old baby all became too much for Arthur. At the beginning of September he left Ivy and the child and once more headed for the Lake District with his newly-acquired lightweight tent stuffed into his knapsack. He camped in various spots, including the Lanehead garden. We can only imagine what Ivy thought of such desertion. While Ransome was camped on Peel Island, the proofs of his book on Poe arrived at Lanehead. Ursula Collingwood, the youngest member of the family, cycled down to the lake shore and, with the carefully wrapped proofs tied to her head, swam across to the island. After going through the 160 pages together, Ursula swam back with the proofs corrected.

When the Collingwoods left Lanehead for

The Manor Farm at Hatch in Wiltshire where the Ransomes lived for two years before Arthur fled to Russia in 1913. (Ted Alexander)

Reading at the beginning of the Michaelmas term, Ivy, Tabitha and Tabitha's Jamaican nurse joined Arthur for a period of house-sitting, during which Ivy helped him in compiling his two anthologies, *The Book of Friendship* and *The Book of Love*. For a while there seems to have been a period of peace and love in their relationship. According to Ransome's diary, he was suffering at this time from regular bouts of the blues and stomach upsets. Was he still hankering after the Collingwood girls?

There followed three unsettled months in Chelsea before they rented an isolated mediaeval farmhouse at Hatch in Wiltshire, with convenient access to Bournemouth. Mrs Walker made the occasional visit to Hatch, but more frequently Ivy went to Bournemouth, believing it was better that way.

Arthur was always off somewhere else, visiting friends, going to see his publisher, or staying with his mother. Ivy rarely attempted to stop him, though clearly she was unhappy about his roaming away from home. She had been used to plenty of attention and could be quite demanding and theatrical just when he wanted to sit at his typewriter or slip away and go fishing or play billiards. For his part, Arthur did not always appreciate Ivy's needs, nor the fact that when he was away, she was lonely and isolated, being stuck in a large house in the country with few neighbours. Ivy liked visitors, so he invited Dora to stay at their new home. In February 1912 she recorded some observations after a week with the Ransomes:

My godchild is charming, and I am getting to like her mother very much. It is a quaint and unconventional household. There is one maid and Ivy does a lot of the housework, and I help as much as I can. I intended to stay about ten days, but they have persuaded me to a full fortnight. I like Ivy. I don't quite understand her yet; she seems to be several entirely different people at different times. But she is so very devoted to Arthur, and is obviously so very ready to give up anything and everything for his sake, and I like her for that. She really loves him. She was telling me last evening how she first met him, in what her parents and his mother thought was a very improper way, and how he proposed to her before he had known her for half an hour.

Dora noticed that Arthur kept out of the way a lot. He was probably engaged on the next piece of literary criticism — on Oscar Wilde — which was to land him in the High Court in April 1913, defending a libel action brought by Lord Alfred Douglas. Completely out of his depth, Ransome regretted bitterly that he had ever written the book and spent several months of anguish while awaiting the trial. The court hearing lasted four days before Ransome was acquitted, but the experience left its scars and he resolved never to write anything which might possibly lead to a similar experience.

Over the next year the marriage was to deteriorate further, with disagreements on both sides. On one occasion they sat down and talked out their differences. 'Long intimate talk – both very happy', Ransome wrote, but it was not to last. Fully committed to his writing, Ransome had been reading philosophers Kant, Paracelsus and Schopenhauer. He was working on the collection of essays which were to be published in 1913 under the title of *Portraits and Speculations*. In the opening essay, 'Art for Life's sake' we have Ransome reflecting on the nature of art:

> Art is itself life. Its function is to increase our consciousness of life, to make us more than wise or sensitive, to transform us from beings overwhelmed by the powerful stream of unconscious living to beings dominating that stream, to change us from objects acted upon by life to joyful collaborators in that reaction.

Nothing in their relationship or Ivy's behaviour was going to get in the way of Ransome's determination to succeed as a writer! From his point of view, she was very possessive and would not leave him alone to get on with his work. Eventually, in May 1913, he decided to make a break and set off, ostensibly for Stockholm, but effectively for Russia. It had taken a little over four years for the prediction of friends and the worst fears of Mrs Walker to be realised.

Chapter Three
ESCAPE TO RUSSIA

By the time Arthur Ransome left Ivy and Tabitha in the late spring of 1913, his enthusiasm for fairy stories had been rekindled by Post Wheeler's translation of twelve Russian folk tales, *Russian Wonder Tales*, published in 1912. In Russia, there was a rich tradition of folklore; stories passed down orally from generation to generation, and unknown to English readers. Ransome wanted to 'gather' these stories first-hand so that he could make his own collection for English children. What was more, he had friends who could help him become established in Russia where Ivy, who had no passport, would have difficulty in following him.

Even so, when he boarded the steamer for Copenhagen, he probably had no more than a half-formed plan for escape. Upon arrival in St Petersburg some weeks later, he set himself to learn Russian with the aid of a set of graded children's readers. He was always modest about his linguistic achievements, claiming only that it was easy. Few of those who have tried would agree with him. Ransome's facility with written and spoken Russian was to prove invaluable a few years later when he was able to attend high level meetings and report on the events of the Revolution.

His first visit to Eastern Europe lasted three months, and much of that time was spent by the Gulf of Finland and in the Baltic Provinces. In spite of having made some sort of a break with Ivy, by the end of October he had come to 'a very unsatisfactory agreement' with his wife and was back at Hatch. He spent most of the winter there, working on a biography of Robert Louis Stevenson, whom he so admired and with whom he had much in common. At the same time, he was engaged on two more books for children: a lively rhyming version of *Aladdin*, which was published in an extravagantly illustrated edition in 1919, and a strange allegorical tale, *The Blue Treacle*, which had to wait 80 years before it was published under the aegis of The Arthur Ransome Society.

He returned to Russia in May 1914, armed with a commission to write a guidebook to St Petersburg, and upon his departure the unfinished Stevenson manuscript, comprising almost 400 pages, was deposited in a London bank where it remained until after Tabitha's death in 1991. A few short extracts were printed in The *Independent on Sunday* in 1994, among them a passage on *Treasure Island*, in which Ransome cast objective criticism aside and wrote:

> I open it to remind myself of some little detail of technique, and from that page I read willy-nilly to the end. My edition is dated 1894 and is one of the fifty-second thousand. In the last twenty years I must have read it twenty times. And now I cannot write of it as a literary achievement. No; I speculate upon the fortunes of Long John...I wonder what became of the three maroons who were left on the island as a punishment for their wicked mutiny. I hear Long John cursing the flies on his large red face, or see him smoking silently with Captain Smollett, as in the picture of the loghouse door. And then there are delicious perilous moments, up the mast with hands climbing from below, and jerking his dagger murderously through the air to pin me — or was it Jim Hawkins? — to the mast.

The guide to St Petersburg was completed in a frantic eight weeks of visiting cathedrals, museums and galleries. By the time it was finished, Europe was plunging into war. Ransome found it all 'extraordinarily interesting' and described the situation in a letter to his mother before returning to England:

> Thousands and thousands of reservists in their coloured blouses are camped all over the town, waiting for uniforms before being sent off to the various fronts. There is no music, no cheering, or very little and that rather horrible and unreal. There is a feeling of steady and resigned determination, which looks very well.

The Under-Secretary for Foreign Affairs, Francis Acland, who was an old friend of the Ransome family, persuaded Arthur not to enlist, as his poor eyesight would have been a handicap in the trenches, and urged him instead to find some newspaper work for which his knowledge of Russian could be put to use. While Ransome had never intended to become a journalist, the friends and contacts he had made in Russia before the outbreak of war especially fitted him for the role. But by then the major newspapers had already appointed their war correspondents and it was not until the end of the year, after Acland had obtained a commission for him to write a *History of Russia*, that he was allowed to return to St Petersburg. Michael Lykiardopoulos (Lyki), the secretary of the Moscow Art Theatre, who had met Ransome in England in connection with a Russian translation of his book on Oscar Wilde, introduced him to the artistic fraternity where he became as much at home as he had been in Edwardian bohemia in London. The proposed history book was never written, but Lyki introduced him to Harold Williams, a greatly respected writer and observer, who advised him to go to Moscow where he could learn much more about Russia than by staying where he was.

In Moscow Ransome found a city facing 'both east and west' and during the four weeks that he spent there, felt that he was living in a 'magic world'. In spite of being unprepared for the freezing temperature, he revelled in his new surroundings and was full of enthusiasm when he wrote to Dora Collingwood shortly after arrival:

> Jan 14. New Year's Day in Russia. Last night I went to one of the cathedrals in the Kremlin, and lost a hat and a glove in the tightest packed crowd I have ever been in... Afterwards I walked along the edge of the hill, looking down from the Kremlin over the frozen river and then went to the house of some Russian friends, and drank non-alcoholic drinks and ate smoked salmon till about three in the morning...I would love to write a story about the old Moscow of Ivan the Terrible. Perhaps I shall, when I know something about it. It's the most historical feeling place I know.

Before returning to St Petersburg, he managed to join the peasants who were fishing in a large hole in the frozen river beside the walls of the Kremlin. Fishing, he said, always calmed and focussed his mind, and there were times when it provided a welcome addition to the scant supplies in his larder. But living in Moscow also had its less pleasant moments, as he explained in a letter to his mother:

> Last night I killed three unmentionable insects, and spent about five sleepless hours in switching the light on and off in the hope of a larger bug. They are large and flat and odorous, and they are imported, I fancy, from the dreadful little hole in the kitchen where the servants sleep.

Perhaps it was this invasion of bugs that he was remembering when he wrote a parody on Wordsworth:

> Oh bugs delight to itch and bite
> In every town I know;
> But when they want society
> To Petersburg they go.
> In regiments they cross the floor
> And climb upon the bed;
> Play hide and seek among my toes
> And rest upon my head.
> In other towns you meet a bug,
> Two bugs, or maybe three,
> But here you meet a million bugs
> In joyous company.
> I scratch with lust,
> I scratch with haste;
> Kindly imagine me,
> As scratch by scratch I punctuate
> My sad extemporee.

Back in St Petersburg, Ransome spent a laborious

The large block of flats on the corner of Glinka Street in St Petersburg where Ransome had his room. It was this room which was raided by the secret police in 1923 when they removed and burnt all his possessions except his fishing rod and a coffee-grinder that were saved by his landlady. (Ted Alexander)

month writing almost 60,000 words of a full-length historical novel, *The Elixir of Life*. He was encouraged in this project by Hugh Walpole, an old friend from his Chelsea days, who was now working for the Red Cross in Russia. The story, which is told in the first person, is about a foppish young man who, having quarrelled with his guardian, falls in with a 200-year-old stranger surviving by means of regular doses of the elixir of life. Needless to say, there is a 20-year-old heroine for the young man to rescue, and after all the melodrama is over, the story ends with reconciliation and a return to Westmorland and comfortable north country names like Bigland, Newby and Swainson. The bad-tempered old guardian is the most interesting character in the book:

My uncle died some six years later, thanking God

that his illness had come upon him at the end of the trout season, instead of at the beginning. He had the satisfaction of making a fisherman of me, and of fastening a bent pin on the end of a thread, and seeing his first great-nephew catch a minnow.

As soon as the book was off his hands, Ransome went back to working on *Old Peter's Russian Tales*. For relaxation, he was able to leave his flat in St Petersburg from time to time and retreat to the country, where he stayed with the Harold Williams family at their estate beside the Volkhov River. There he could write for part of the day and then go fishing to his heart's content. On one occasion, when offering an artificial fly to a number of rising dace and pulling them out of the water one after another, he was attacked by 'clouds of poisonous mosquitoes, who made a most unholy mess of every visible part of me.'

The twenty stories in *Old Peter's Russian Tales* were completed in June 1915 and dedicated to Barbara Collingwood. In an explanatory note at the beginning of the book, he assures his readers that: 'In Russia hardly anybody is too old for fairy stories, and I have even heard soldiers on their way to war talking of very wise and very beautiful princesses as they drank their tea by the side of the road.'

One of the book's strengths lies in the device Ransome used to make it more accessible to English children, allowing old Peter to tell the stories to his orphaned grandchildren, Maroosia and Vanya, so providing continuity and a means of conveying necessary explanations which would otherwise have become tedious. The folk tales called for a simple, concise and energetic style, far removed from some of Ransome's more florid and self-conscious earlier work. There are even signs of the Defoe-like economy and attention to detail which was to mark his mature storytelling of later years:

> Then old Peter took his big coat off and lifted down the samovar from the shelf. The samovar is like a big brass tea-urn, with a stout metal tube running through the middle of it in which the fire is lit to make the water boil. When the water boils it is poured through the tap at the bottom on to tea-leaves in the teapot, and the pot is set on the top of the samovar. A little jet of steam rises through a tiny hole in the lid of the samovar, which hums like a bee and makes one feel extra warm and snug when the weather is cold. Old Peter threw in the lighted sticks and charcoal, and made a draught to draw the heat, and then set the samovar on the table with the little fire crackling inside. Then he cut some big lumps of black bread. Then he took a great saucepan full of soup, that was simmering on the stove, and emptied it into a big wooden bowl. Then he went to the wall where, on three nails, hung three wooden spoons, deep like ladles. There were one big spoon for old Peter; and two little spoons, one for Vanya and one for Maroosia.

The Times Literary Supplement's reviewer was not impressed: 'The tales, though they are second-rate literary matter, should read aloud well.' Reviewing the book again almost twenty years later, the paper was much more gracious in its appraisal. 'It would be impossible to overpraise these simple, humorous and moral stories...'

That summer Ransome began to suffer from severe stomach cramps and ever more painful piles. Eventually, in August, an operation was advised. He wrote to his mother saying that he thought it would cost about £29 — less than in England. He begged her not to tell Ivy, whom he thought might fly to his bedside. The operation was all very unpleasant; the anaesthetics did not work properly and he was in great pain for three sleepless days and nights. He had not fully recovered when he was asked to stand in for the *Daily News*' Russia correspondent who had fallen ill. Ransome's career as a journalist began with Harold Williams delivering his first few cables to the telegraph office while he was still not well enough to get out and about. He himself saw little future in it. 'I am no good as a journalist and never shall be', he wrote to his mother. Whatever his misgivings, when it became clear that the Liberal *Daily News* correspondent would not recover, Ransome was offered his job. Recognising that this new development gave him a good reason to return to England to complete his convalescence, Ransome left St Petersburg on 18th September to visit the *Daily News* office in London. He agreed to become their Russia correspondent on condition that he might be allowed to return home at least once each year and that he should be able to use his judgment whether to remain in St Petersburg or move closer to any of the action.

By the beginning of November he was back in Russia, still in a poor way with anaemia and headaches. The city had been renamed Petrograd, as St Petersburg was thought to sound altogether too Germanic. Most of his time was spent in assembling his reports, developing his contacts and calling on Robert Bruce Lockhart, the flamboyant British Consul at the Anglo-Russian Bureau which Ransome had helped to set up. Lockhart recalled Ransome's visits when he would arrive puffing fiercely at his pipe, a bundle of books under his arm and a large revolver at his side, looking for all the world like 'a cross between a professor and a bandit'. It was all most stimulating, as he told his mother:

> I say, it's all very well my grumbling about being worked off my head and feet. I work absolutely continuously all day and through a very long day. But the point is that with my improving health, I both thrive on it, and like it. I enjoy it like fun. It will be like returning to a thoroughly artificial existence when the war ends, or my job ends, and I come back to getting up late, and having nothing to do but a

Gambolling in the lane near Hatch with Tabitha during his visit to England in the autumn of 1917 at the time the October Revolution was taking place in Russia.

book with almost unlimited time to get it done in, and half the day spent in slacking about.

In March 1916 Ransome was given permission to visit the front as a war correspondent. He spent a month at the South Western Army headquarters at Berditchev. One night, while walking with a Russian soldier, he almost blundered into the German lines, but stopped on hearing voices. He contrived to be flown over the battle zone and, on returning to base, the aircraft was nearly shot down by 'friendly fire'. Always one to champion the underdog, he was full of admiration for the Russian soldiers who were holding the front against an enemy which was far better equipped and supplied.

Ransome was on the point of returning to England in August when Rumania entered the war on the side of the Allies. The *Daily News* instructed him to go to Bucharest, which he was able to reach after an unauthorised journey aboard a munitions train. While Zeppelins were bombing the capital, he was not allowed to visit the

Transylvanian front, where things were going badly. He came close to death when he was sent flying by the blast from bombs jettisoned at the edge of the Black Sea. Nevertheless he did manage to send a few articles home in the diplomatic bag before returning to Petrograd.

At the end of October Ransome left for England and a much-needed break. He thought that he had a chance of being appointed to the University of Leeds as Professor of Russian Studies and spoke to the Vice-Chancellor, but apparently without success. He also visited his mother and the Collingwoods, and following a round of talks with Government Ministers he set off for Russia for a fifth time.

During intervals in his work of assembling despatches for the *Daily News*, he now made regular visits to the Duma (the Russian Parliament). By the middle of March, after Lenin's arrival in Petrograd, serious disturbances were erupting in the city. Ransome was able to witness a battle for the prison next door from the window of his flat. In the riotous turmoil he was fortunate to survive when a grenade was dropped from the roof of a building into the street below. For a while he was kept frantically busy, sometimes sending three cables a day with rapidly changing news. He had little understanding of Socialism and for a while was carried away by his enthusiasm for the Revolution. In some accounts of that time he appears as a sentimental romantic, 'kindly and childlike', yet his reporting is sharp and his voice clear, even when expressed in telegraphic shorthand.

Jan 3 1917
News death rasputin passed mouth mouth petrograd saturday stop

April 8 1917
most important anglo russian relations that britain should not be rushed as to attitude russian nation towards war stop would be dangerous to allow wish to be father of thought when choose to what voices britain should listen in new vociferous chorus ungagged russia stop

After the first uprising, things quietened down and Ransome continued to report on regular visits to

The Women's Battalion of 1917 who were known as Amazons. They were mostly recruited from among the increasing number of war widows. Were these young Russian soldiers the inspiration for the war-like Nancy?

the Duma. By October it seemed as if there would be time to make a quick visit to England before there were any more dramatic events, and so he missed the opportunity to witness the October Revolution at first hand.

While he was away from home, Ransome always made a point of keeping in touch with his young daughter Tabitha, writing amusingly illustrated letters to his 'Wooly Ba Ba' and signing them 'Dor Dor'. He would visit Ivy and Tabitha during his brief periods in England, and there were attempts to patch things up between them. In spite of his differences with Ivy, Ransome recognised that she was taking good care of his daughter. When the time came for him to depart once more, there was a hurried farewell meeting at King's Cross Station which brought Ransome close to tears. When he wrote to his mother from the train he confessed to be 'not at all keen on the trip this time', and if there had been an offer of a job, he would have been very glad to stay in England. 'Saying good-bye to Tabitha, who was a perfect darling...nearly made me weep.' The response is in stark contrast to a verse he had sent to his mother in July 1916:

Oh, once I loved the sewing-maids.
And once I loved the cooks,

But now I'll not love anyone
However sweet she looks.

Such was the deteriorating situation in Eastern Europe it seemed unlikely that Ransome would be allowed to re-enter Russia. However Lord Robert Cecil, the Under-Secretary for Foreign Affairs, had given him a diplomatic bag for Stockholm, which ensured that he could at least reach Sweden. From there he was able to return to Petrograd before the end of the year.

The city was in chaos, as the inexperienced Bolsheviks set about government. Within a few days Ransome had met both Lenin and Trotsky, and for a while he saw them almost daily. Trotsky was the organisational genius among the Bolshevik leaders, and it was from his office in the Smolny Institute, a former girls' school but now the revolutionary headquarters, that Ransome began to collect daily notices from Evgenia

Evgenia Shelepina (Leeds U)

Shelepina. He claimed to have met his second wife on 30th December 1917, but it is clear that they already knew one another by sight, and her address appears in his diary under 5th January 1915. It is intriguing to see that the entry, unlike his usual habit, does not contain the name. At the beginning of 1915 Evgenia was 20, but Ransome tells us very little about her, contenting himself with, '...the tall jolly girl whom later on I was to marry and to whom I owe the happiest years of my life.' In a letter to Tabitha, written in May 1918, she was: 'a big girl, as big as Dor Dor, who carries a revolver and a sword and is a fierce revolutionary.'

Evgenia was Trotsky's 'very able' assistant who regularly saw Ransome when she handed out bulletins from Trotsky's office. They developed the habit of walking together to catch the tramcar back to the city centre. In his *Autobiography* he tells how a fatal accident nearly befell Evgenia as she boarded a tramcar which began to move before she had her foot on the platform, dragging

her along as she clung to the handrail. Though it was years before they would admit as much, the incident made them realise the strength of their feelings for one another.

The Shelepins were a very proper Tzarist family who lived close to the Imperial Palace at Gatchina. Evgenia's father, Peter, was the Tzar's curator for a number of institutions, including the hospital, the church, an old people's home and a school. Before entering the Imperial service, he had been required to sign an affidavit (which exists today) declaring that he had never been connected with a political group or a religious sect. His two daughters, Evgenia and her younger sister Iraida, were educated at a prestigious girls' school in Gatchina which had a name for very high academic standards, especially in history, literature and foreign languages. How Peter's eldest daughter became a revolutionary leader's personal assistant remains a mystery. While Trotsky was away negotiating peace terms with Germany at Brest-Litovsk, it was she who ran his office in his absence. Trotsky had helped to organise the Bolshevik seizure of power, and Evgenia must have been aware of many of the momentous decisions.

During the months that followed, Ransome seems to have become closer to the Bolshevik leaders than any other Westerner at that time. He was invited to attend the 'Soviet' (revolutionary council of Workers and Soldiers' Deputies) and important meetings of the Executive Committee of the Soviet. Because he was trusted by the Bolsheviks as the correspondent most likely to present them in the best possible light in the West, Ransome became, to all intents and purposes, a member of the British Diplomatic Mission.

His closest contact among the Soviets was Karl Radek, whom Trotsky had put in charge of the Press Bureau at the Commissariat for Foreign affairs. Like Ransome, Radek was a keen observer of human nature and apt to collect around him those of a somewhat eccentric character. As part of his official duties, he intercepted a parcel sent on by Ransome from Stockholm and was at once curious to meet a foreign reporter whose personal belongings should consist of 'Shakespeare, a folding chess-board and chessmen, and a collection of books on elementary navigation, fishing, chess

The Smolny Institute in St Petersburg, a former girls' school, was the Bolshevik headquarters at the time of the Revolution. Here Ransome called to collect the daily news bulletin from Evgenia and to walk with her to the tram after work. (Ted Alexander)

and folklore.' Trotsky himself saw to it that both Ransome and Lockhart were furnished with a pass to leave the city whenever they wished to go on fishing expeditions, so gaining them the respect of armed guards at every city exit. Mastermind Lenin was also a fisherman, and Lockhart regrets in his memoirs that he missed the chance to use the subject to soften up the 'not unkind, but politically cold genius'. At least Ransome managed to get Lenin to the chess-board, though some years later he told Malcolm Muggeridge (then a correspondent with the *Manchester Guardian*) that, unlike Litvinov, Lenin proved to be a rather poor player.

A remarkable 18-year-old Polish girl, Lola Kinel, became friends with Ransome at this time through a shared interest in books and chess. They met on a train in which she and her sister were returning home to Petrograd after a holiday in America. In her autobiography *Under Five Eagles*, she described Ransome as 'tall, dressed in a Russian military coat, though without any insignia, and a fur cap. He had long red moustaches, completely concealing his mouth, and humorous, twinkling eyes.' From her autobiography it is possible to picture Ransome's room. One

corner was dedicated to working and contained a large desk and a typewriter. The desk was covered with papers and was very dusty because he forbade the maids to touch it. In another corner a screen partly concealed a bed, a night table and a dresser. In the middle of the room was an old sofa and a round table with some chairs. What impressed Lola most were the books. They were everywhere, heaped in rows on the furniture, on chairs, on the sofa and even on the floor. Scattered among the books Lola used to find his old, torn and soiled socks.

Ransome encouraged Lola Kinel to take the side of the revolutionaries:

AK (Ransome) was very enthusiastic about the Bolsheviks and I did not want to give him any satisfaction on this point. My neutral attitude both puzzled and irritated him.

'All the young people I know are working for the Revolution. How can you be so different and stand aside?' he would say.

'I don't know whether the Bolsheviks are right, AK,' I would reply. 'You are very romantic. You are just carried away. You don't know anything about socialism or economics.'

He would grow almost furious at this — as far as was possible with his kindly and childlike nature.

In March 1918 the entire Bolshevik Government left for Moscow where Trotsky, who was Commissar for War, began to form the Red Army. Amazingly, Trotsky's St Petersburg office — which includes Evgenia's work area — has survived. Eighty years after Ransome's visits members of the Arthur Ransome Society were able to enter the former Bolshevik Headquarters. Ted Alexander and Tatiana Verizhnikova, who have made a study of the time Ransome spent in Russia, were led past the armed guards who stand outside the Smolny Institute and taken to the top floor of the building where the guide unlocked the offices that have remained unused since the government departed. Evgenia's typewriter was still in place on her desk, the table lamp and other furniture left as if she might be returning for work the following morning.

Ransome followed the Bolsheviks to Moscow and remained there until, with the approach of landings by the Allies at Archangel in support of the anti-Bolshevik White Army, his position, like that of all British subjects, was at risk. In anticipation of possible difficulties if the White Army should enter Moscow, he arranged for Evgenia to be put on his passport. They had already decided to live together, although Ivy had made it clear that she would not agree to a divorce. As it turned out, Evgenia never used any passport or documents other than her own Russian ones up to the time of her marriage to Arthur. In late July they agreed that it would be better for Evgenia to leave Russia, and it was arranged for her to become a secretary with the Russian Legation in Stockholm.

Firmly against any Allied armed intervention in the civil war, Ransome felt he had to counter the outpourings of a generally hostile British press, and in so doing, he fell foul of the Foreign Office, which regarded him with some distrust. His reputation as a 'Red journalist' was well established by then and secret service reports, which Bruce Lockhart showed to him, denounced him as a 'Bolshevik agent'. For his part, Lockhart thought of Ransome as 'a visionary, whose imagination had been fired by the revolution' and 'an incorrigible romanticist, who could spin a fairy-tale out of nothing.'

By early August, with his position becoming increasingly unsustainable, Ransome joined Evgenia in neutral Sweden, where they set up their first home together in rooms close to the sea-approaches to the city. When the armistice was signed, Sweden broke off relations with Russia and expelled the Russian Legation where Evgenia had been working.

At this time Ransome's letters to his mother were very different to the exuberant outpourings that he had sent two years earlier in the winter of 1916:

The *Daily News* sent me some tobacco, including four blocks of black plug, guaranteed to kill at ten yards. I cut up some, stuffed it in a clay pipe, and at the first puff I was back at home drinking beer with Lascelles Abercrombie in the 'Hark to Melody' by Haverthwaite. Then I was talking to the charcoal burners who used to bake clay pipes for me in the wood above Coniston. Then I was in a good old stinking Furness Railway third class carriage with a lot of miners going oop Millom way. It's no good; the Russian Revolution has failed utterly in altering me personally. Once I get a little peace and quiet and get my sketch of the development of the revolution written, I shall write FINIS and fetch politics a good boost with a boot in the latter parts, and return with no regrets whatever to pen, ink, tobacco, fishing and the lake country... I would so like to have a couple of months to spend on a new children's book... Revolts may come, revolts may go, but brats go on for ever.

Just before Christmas he wrote to his mother again:

The *Daily News* is quite evidently hankering to send me to Berlin, but I'm not having any, thank you. I've had the unpopularity of telling the truth about one damned revolution, and nothing will induce me to touch another at the end of a barge pole.

The pair remained in their rooms until January 1919, when they too were expelled. With his marriage to Ivy undissolved, Arthur and Evgenia felt that they could not live openly as man and wife in England and it is very unlikely that the Foreign Office would have allowed Evgenia to enter the country. Instead they decided to return to Russia, where he could turn his newspaper articles into a book called *Six Weeks in Russia*. Evgenia had no trouble in finding employment with the Department of Education in Moscow, and in March 1919, with his book completed, Ransome managed to slip home to England with an unofficial American mission, only to be met at King's Cross Station by a plain-clothes policeman who took him to Scotland Yard to be interrogated by head of the Special Branch, Sir Basil Thomson.

I was shown into Sir Basil Thomson's room and asked to sit down in the famous chair where so many criminals had sat before me. Sir Basil, extremely grim, looked hard at me. After a moment's silence, he said, 'Now, I want to know what your politics are.'

'Fishing,' I replied.

He stared. 'Just what do you mean by that?'

I told him the exact truth, that in England I had never had any political views whatever, that in Russia I believed that this very fact had let me get a clearer view of the revolution than I could otherwise have got, that I now had one clear political opinion, which was that Intervention was a disastrous mistake, and that I hoped it would come to an end and so release me to turn to my ordinary interests.

'Fishing?' he said.

'We are very near the beginning of the season,' I replied.

A few years ago a claim was made in *The Times* newspaper by the Cambridge historian, Christopher Andrew, that recently released KGB documents disclosed Ransome as indeed an agent of the Cheka and 'the most important secret source of intelligence on British Foreign policy'. The Soviet leaders certainly made use of him for their own ends, but short of any payslips or similar evidence being produced, it is not reasonable to see Ransome as more than a sympathetic observer who saw his role as intermediary.

The Biographical Chronicle of Lenin, published in Russia in 1974, includes three meetings with Ransome. They do not appear to be the records of meetings with a Bolshevik agent. None the less, two extracts throw some light on his usefulness to the Soviet leaders at this time:

23 March 1918
Lenin gave an interview to A. Ransome, the correspondent of the English newspaper *Daily News*, concerning the statement of the British Foreign minister, A.Balfour, made on 14 March 1918 in the House of Commons alleging that Japan is giving aid to Russia in the struggle against Germany.

Between 14th and 22nd February 1919
Lenin talks with the English journalist A. Ransome about the state and prospects of the workers' movement in England and the international importance of the Soviets etc.

Ransome's staunch opposition to British intervention became at odds with the policy of the *Daily News* after its Cadbury proprietors sacked the editor for his pro-Bolshevik views and brought an end to Ransome's association with the newspaper.

Six Weeks in Russia can hardly be called objective reporting, for its intention was to show the Soviet leaders in a good light. Ransome chose to play down the activities of the Cheka, and he was equally careful not to say anything which might result in him being accused of betraying British Government secrets. The book was published in 1919 and sympathetically reviewed in the *Daily Mail* by Hamilton Fyfe, whom Ransome had taught to fish for tench in a horsepond during his time as a correspondent in Russia:

It would be unfair to call Mr. Ransome a Bolshevik. He is no politician. He is an observer...he sees plainly and deplores the mistakes the Bolsheviks have made, such as their suppression of the Constituent Assembly, and he hates as much as any man the brutal deeds done in the name of the Revolution.

An anonymous writer in the *Daily News* was equally supportive:

> Mr Ransome is no blind admirer of Bolshevik Russia. He is only too well aware of human imperfections in general and of Bolshevik failings in particular, but he has imagination, he is not blinded by prejudice, and he can see the eternal and ideal behind the frail and mortal.

The *Manchester Guardian* carried a long review of what it called 'an authentic document...of all the greater value because it advocates nothing and scarcely draws any conclusions...' C.P. Scott, the *Manchester Guardian's* celebrated editor, approved of the book and offered Ransome a free hand if he would go to Russia for the paper. The Foreign Office refused to allow him to leave the country, and he spent a fretful summer in England until Sir Basil Thomson intervened and a Russian visa was granted. With war between the Bolsheviks and the White Russian and Estonian armies at its height, Estonia wanted peace, and Ransome, upon arriving in the capital, Reval, was charged with delivery of a message to the Soviets seeking a settlement.

Reaching Moscow entailed a long and difficult journey which involved crossing the front lines of the opposing armies. Once over the White front line, he approached the trenches of the Red Army, casually puffing at his pipe and hoping that none of the soldiers pointing their rifles in his direction would be given the order to fire. The young officer in command of the troops had orders to shoot anybody crossing the lines.

Ransome cautioned him over a cup of tea with the notion that it might prove to be an imprudent and irrevocable mistake to kill a friend of Lenin's. Instead the officer agreed to send him to his superior, and this stratagem was repeated several times until he reached Moscow. Having successfully secured the essential Bolshevik reply, agreeing terms for an armistice, Ransome and Evgenia returned to Reval.

Before the response could be delivered, they faced another hazardous crossing between the opposing armies, and for part of the journey Evgenia had to travel on a cart, hidden by sacks of potatoes. Due largely to the resourcefulness of Evgenia, who bought their lives with a tea-kettle and the old officer's coat which Ransome still wore, they were able to enter the White Russian territory where they met a troop of White cavalry advancing towards them. The officer in command rushed forward, pulled up his horse and, upon recognising Ransome, exclaimed: 'What luck! Now we can have that game of chess!' The officer had been unlucky to lose a game when they had played some months earlier, and now he wanted the chance of revenge!

Finally they entered Estonia in the autumn of 1919 and delivered the Bolshevik's answer. This was Ransome's most successful mission as a go-between, for the reply that he carried led to the Treaty of Dorpat, and this gained Estonia twenty years of independence from Russia. Over the next ten years Ransome entered Russia from time to time, but it would be fifty years before Evgenia returned to her homeland again.

Chapter Four
BALTIC INTERLUDE

Once safely in Reval on the Baltic coast of Estonia, Ransome collapsed with a particularly virulent attack of the stomach trouble which had plagued him for several years, and what he described as 'brain fever'. With the care of a good Estonian doctor and Evgenia's nursing, he was able to make a steady recovery. The couple took lodgings in a wooden house in the woods near Lodenzee at the head of Lahepe Bay, 40 miles west of Reval. For four years they lived together in Eastern Europe as man and wife until Ivy was prepared to agree to a divorce, and he was free to marry Evgenia and make a home for them in the Lake District.

Living in Estonia, and later in Latvia, Ransome could visit Russia and was able to prepare commentaries on the situation in Eastern Europe without Russian censorship. His work as a Special Correspondent for the *Manchester Guardian* was a much more leisurely occupation than sending hurriedly composed telegrams to the *Daily News*.

He returned to Russia in the spring of 1920 in order to gather material for a book on the economic situation. His romantic view of the revolution, recognised by Bruce Lockhart, is still evident in *The Crisis in Russia*. While in Petrograd, Ransome was able to visit his old rooms, only to find that his collection of newspapers, which he had intended to present to the British Museum, had been burnt by the Communists. In his next letter to his mother, he gave vent to his feelings: '...but to burn it...Forty thousand million dancing devils with pink tails and purple stomach aches.' His landlady had managed to save his favourite fishing rod, but all his other possessions had been stolen.

As soon as spring gave way to summer, Evgenia was introduced to the pleasures of boating. Ransome tried to have a ship's lifeboat brought out from England, and when that did not materialise, he bought a large dinghy and ballasted it with boulders from the beach. With the aid of a newly acquired prismatic compass, the pair set sail from Reval towards Lahepe Bay.

At first the little boat, which they had named *Slug*, dribbled along in a near calm before the light winds gave way to a storm and they were glad of the large stones which did duty as ballast and made *Slug* so very stiff. The storm abated as quickly as it had started, and by midnight they were becalmed. The plan had been to arrive home in time for breakfast, but around four in the morning they anchored and slept on the boulders until eleven. Nothing daunted, they sailed on, finishing their voyage with Ransome wading through the abnormally shallow water of the bay, towing *Slug*. Later he was to admit that it was ridiculous to have taken an open boat for sixty miles tacking along a coast they did not know.

In the summer of 1921, they bought another boat in Reval, which they renamed *Kittywake*. She was even smaller and less seaworthy than *Slug*, and the cabin, which had so attracted them at first, had bunks which proved too narrow for a couple of large folk. That year they made their base at Baltic Port (Paldiski), a few miles west of Lahepe Bay which was really too shallow to keep a boat.

The couple reached Baltic Port after a voyage punctuated by storms and calms lasting twenty-five hours. Finally, with the wind heading them, Ransome had to row the heavy craft into the harbour. It was little wonder that, when they reached their hotel, he fell asleep with his head on the table. *Kittywake* took them only as far as the

Carl Sehmel with the small craft that he looked after in the tiny harbour in a corner of the Stint See Lake at Riga where he met Ransome.

Roogo islands, but they had plans for a yacht in which they could cruise for days on end and spent some time with a yacht designer, Otto Eggers, talking of dream ships fit to be sailed anywhere.

After spending three months at Baltic Port the pair left Estonia and moved to Latvia where they took rooms near the shore of what Ransome called the 'Stint See' lake at Kaiserwald, outside the port of Riga. The local boatbuilder constructed a small fishing dinghy with a leg-of-mutton sail for them to use on the lake. So impressed was Ransome with its builder that he felt he could safely trust him to construct his dream ship, Ransome returned to Eggers in Reval and commissioned him to draw up the plans:

She was to be a cruising boat that one man could

manage if need be, but on which three could manage to live comfortably. She was to have a writing table and a bookcase, a place for a typewriter, broad bunks where a man might lay him down and rest without bruising knee and elbow with each unconsidered movement. She should not be fast, but she should be fit to keep to sea when other little boats were scuttling for shelter. In fact she was to be the boat that every man would wish who likes to move from port to port — a little ship in which, in temperate climates, a man might live from year's end to year's end.

The new boat was to be called *Racundra*, a name Ransome had made up, he and Evgenia became 'Ra und ra'. The letter 'c' came from the first name of Carl Sehmel, his paid hand, and was probably inserted to make the name pronounceable. In Ransome's book, *Racundra's First Cruise*, Sehmel appears as 'The Ancient Mariner', and he was finally immortalised as Peter Duck in the third of the Swallows and Amazons books. Sehmel had

Aboard **Slug** *in Lahepe Bay 1920*

once shipped aboard the *Thermopylae* in the Australian wool trade, but had retired from the sea and was looking after the boats on the Stint See. Ransome told his mother, 'He is very ancient...He wants to sail to England with me next year. He is quite the best sailor in these parts, and I shall be glad to have him if only to pick up hints from him, to polish up what, hitherto, I have been finding out for myself.'

Racundra should have been ready in May 1922, but the sorry story of her building was one of successive delays and revised delivery dates. The summer passed slowly until, in August, Ransome became desperate, seized the boat and took her to the yacht club where he could attend to her himself. After a fortnight's hard work, *Racundra* was pronounced fit to take to sea. The yacht was a shallow draft ketch, nine metres long with a massive beam of three and a half metres and a centreboard. Its proud owner enthused about her cabin

Racundra *in Tangier harbour, where she was based for some years before making the Atlantic crossing that ended when she foundered on a reef off the coast of Venezuela in 1978.* (courtesy Paul Crisp)

but was inclined to gloss over the effects of putting such extravagant accommodation in a nine metres hull, at the same time insisting that she be rigged in such a way as to enable single-handed sailing if necessary. To his mother, he was more forthright: 'She is very easy to manage and so slow on her helm that I have plenty of time to do things while she takes care of herself. But SLOW. My word. Something terrific. Our motion has a stately leisuredness about it that is reminiscent of the Middle Ages.'

Evgenia appears in *Racundra's First Cruise* as 'the Cook', whose life aboard was a constant round of preparing the next meal and clearing up after the last. 'Of the three of us, the Cook, without a doubt, was the one who worked her passage.' At that time the Ransomes had a cat called Tom and a metre-long grass snake from Moscow called Curobokos which had a passion for frogs. The snake travelled in a large jam jar and liked to curl itself round the base of their teapot. The story of how the snake would curl round Evgenia's bosoms when she was asleep on her bunk, was handed down in the Sehmel family.

They finally left Riga early one morning towards the end of August and sailed north for the island of Runo where a few Swedish seal-hunting inhabitants lived a life that had been untouched by the twentieth century and were still using eighteenth-century flintlock rifles. Ransome's ability to colour straightforward events with imaginative romance, which was to become the hallmark of *Swallows and Amazons*, shines out from his description of their landing; 'Our landing on Runo was like a page from *Robinson Crusoe* or a child's dream of desert islands....Man, should he appear, might be of any kind. Almost, we looked up at the tree tops for pygmies with their poisoned arrows, and watched the trunks of the trees for the feathers of one of Fenimore Coopers's Indian braves.'

The anchorage off Runo was an exposed one, and after a brief spell ashore they set sail again for Reval. In spite of discovering that their compass could not be relied upon, Ransome successfully piloted *Racundra* through the islands and sailed on, hoping to reach Baltic Port before nightfall. The wind increased and *Racundra* passed the test magnificently until the jaws of the mainsail gaff broke. They began to tack towards Baltic Port under staysail and mizzen alone. The Ancient Mariner was all for keeping on, but he was overruled by his skipper who turned about for the open sea.

There followed a 'wild, but in a curious way, rather enjoyable night,' as Ransome began to bellow 'Spanish Ladies' and 'Summer is acumen in' and 'John Peel' — which eventually brought Evgenia up the companion way.

> She asked, with real inquiry, 'Are we going to be drowned before morning?'
> I leaned forward from the steering well and shouted, 'Why?'
> 'Because I have two thermos flasks full of hot coffee. If we are, we may as well drink them both. If not, I'll keep one till tomorrow.'

They kept one. When it grew light, the Ancient made a temporary repair of the jaws, and under full sail once more, they braved a rainstorm and reached Reval the following day in time for supper.

Eggers spent five days putting to rights some of the makeshift workmanship of *Racundra's* builders before she sailed for Helsingfors (Helsinki). Evgenia remained in Reval to make room for the former Estonian ambassador in London, who was in a hurry to reach Helsingfors and had arranged to sail with Ransome and the Ancient Mariner.

Having arrived in Helsingfors and delivered the ambassador, they had the unreliable compass adjusted before the long, cold night haul back to Reval in order to collect Evgenia for the return passage to Riga. Ransome's confidence had soared and he was determined to attempt to sail against the wind through the narrow channel between the Islands of Worms and Nukke. The Ancient Mariner told him that this was something the local seamen never attempted. Ransome went to the bows to look for shoals while the Ancient Mariner took the helm. Apart from one horrible moment when the centreboard touched bottom, they sailed through without incident. 'A gorgeous day'

Ransome wrote in the log.

Evgenia joined them at Reval and they hoped for a speedy passage to Riga, but the equinoctual gales delayed their progress for five days while they waited at Werder (Virtsu) in Estonia until a change of wind to the north-west finally drove them back to Riga.

Ransome had taken eighty photographs and had the material for a 'pretty jolly little book.' Whenever he could, he worked on the book during a month-long stay in Russia and a flying visit to England to set in motion arrangements for a divorce. *Racundra's First Cruise* was completed in January 1923 and published shortly afterwards. Reissued in several editions over the years, it has achieved the status of a yachting classic.

The cruise itself is related with the pride of a successful apprentice navigator, though much of the book is concerned with the remote island communities which had not experienced the Great War. There is also a chapter on Reval and another on the changes twelve months had brought to Baltic Port once the Russian navy began to take over:

> The harbourmaster is too busy to sail his little skiff. The few shops have already multiplied to a dozen or more, and whereas in the old days the harbour-master's wife was only sometimes willing to give lodging to those whom she counted her friends, there is now a regular hotel, the rooms of which are full of busy, serious people, interested in the new activity of the port. Big steamers with steel cables will soon leave no room for the schooners, and little ships like Racundra and Kittywake will never again find Baltic Port the delightful lazy anchorage that it was a year ago.

The simplicity and clarity of the writing, which emerged with *Old Peter's Russian Tales*, had reached maturity.

> On the shingle below the fort where the women sit with their children, fastening small flat stones as sinkers to the bottom of the nets, I saw a German mine being put to a purpose precisely opposite to that for which it was intended. The fishermen were building a new boat. Her keel was laid and they were putting on the planking. They were busy steaming the planks and the boiler was a German mine, emp-

tied of its explosives and neatly fitted over a small furnace of stones from the beach. How they had managed to get the explosives out I do not know, but here was the mine with a good fire under it, boiling away like a domestic kettle, and being used for making boats instead of their destruction.

Early in 1923, Ransome went back to Moscow in search of material for articles on post-revolutionary literature. While he was away, their house in Riga burnt down. Evgenia would almost certainly have perished in the fire had she not been awaked by their cat Tom. They lost *Racundra's* gear and almost all their personal possessions in the blaze, and what was not burnt was stolen by the firemen.

Ransome returned to England once more that spring, visiting the offices of the *Manchester Guardian* where he secured an agreement to receive a regular retaining fee rather than continue being paid for piece-work. The deal gave him the security he had lost when he left the *Daily News*. But before he could quit politics altogether, he was to become embroiled in a situation which appeared to be heading for a fracture in Anglo-Russian relations. The Foreign Secretary in London had written an uncompromising note to the Russians, making a number of demands which, if not met, would lead to a break in trade and possibly to war itself. More, he had forbidden Robert Hodgson, the head of the Mission in Moscow, to discuss its content with the Russians when he personally delivered the ultimatum. Ransome, who was a good friend of Hodgson, visited the Kremlin and engineered a meeting between the two sides in spite of the Foreign Secretary's insistence that no such discussion should take place. As a result, the Russians were persuaded to make the sort of response which would ensure that there would be no breakdown in diplomatic relations.

On returning to Riga, Ransome engaged the Ancient Mariner once more, and they set sail in *Racundra* in mid-July with plans for a cruise to Petrograd. However, it was already quite late in the season, and they eventually decided that the risk of being held up by south-west winds was too great, so instead they took *Racundra* for a short cruise among the Finnish Islands before returning to Reval where *Racundra* was laid up for the winter.

Soon after that the *Manchester Guardian* was anxious for its Special Correspondent to go to Moscow to arrange for some articles to be written for the newspaper's Economic Supplement. He was still there when Lenin died in January 1924. After a brief visit to Evgenia in February, Ransome set off for England to secure the final settlement of his divorce. The ship in which he sailed became trapped in the ice near the island of Bornholm, and when the food ran out, Ransome and a couple of crew members managed to reach land in a small boat and purchase a sheep. Almost immediately, the ship broke free of the ice and, although damaged, was able to limp on to London.

Once he had arrived in England Ransome visited his lawyer. More consultations followed, and it was several weeks before the divorce proceedings were completed. During that time Arthur wrote numerous loving and encouraging letters to Evgenia, addressing her variously as Jenny, Dearest Topsy, Zhennia and dear Old Woman. Evgenia was lonely and miserable, particularly after the death of their cat. She had seen little of Arthur since the autumn. She was not such a good correspondent as he, but when she did write, her letters were to the point: 'It is too awful to think of you losing your books and if until now I tried to believe with you that W [short for Wiltshire, where Ivy was living] doesn't know what she is doing – I can't do it any longer. She knows only too well how to hurt most painfully. She is cruel and that is most unpleasant for me, because I do not think I am worth so much. Poor dear Charlie.' (Evgenia called Ransome Charlie after Charlie Chaplin).

By the terms of what he called a 'frantically bad' divorce settlement, Ransome had to allow Ivy to keep his considerable library as well as paying her a third of his income. Years before, he had been unable to screw himself up to face an explosive scene with Ivy in order to escape from their engagement, and now, in spite of the encouragement from friends, he shrank from simply calling and taking his books. Evgenia was typically forthright: 'It seems to me that the only thing for you to do (if after all they won't accept your offers) is to hire a motor lorry, buy plenty of wooden boxes, take one or two of your friends with you for help and go straight to Wiltshire and pack all your books and take them straight on board *Baltabor* and sail to Riga, books and all'.

Ransome replied shortly before the final settlement: 'Never mind. We will collect a library of our own fast enough, and I shall get a lot from home as well. And anyway, I have done my best writing without any books at all (*Old Peter's Russian Tales* and *Racundra's First Cruise*) and I want to do that sort of book in future. Books that depend on the writing and not on knowledge of other books.'

In the middle of April the years of waiting came to an end, and Ransome returned to Riga a free man. A couple of days later the pair set off for Reval to make arrangements for the wedding and to attend to *Racundra's* fitting out. Finally, Arthur Michell Ransome and Evgenia Petrovna Shelepina were married on 8th May 1924 at the British Consulate in Reval.

Those who remember Evgenia tell of her large size, her strength, her deep voice and her pronounced accent which some found hard to understand. Friends were greeted with a warm hug, and some delicacy that she had just bought or cooked would be thrust upon them. They recall that she was practical and down-to-earth as she prodded Ransome in his more airy-fairy moods. She was hasty tempered, quick to form judgments, argumentative and given to exaggeration. She joined her husband in fishing, sailed with him, nursed him and shared his love of nature — although she thought nothing of clubbing to death a trespassing mouse, something the kindly Ransome would never have done.

They took *Racundra* to sea once more, calling at Baltic Port and Riga before setting off at the beginning of August on a gentle cruise up the Dvina (Dougara) River. Finally, they set off for England in November.

No sooner had they arrived in London than the *Manchester Guardian* wanted Ransome to go to Egypt to report on the political situation there. No doubt he was unwilling to go, but the newspaper had refused to renew his retaining fee after the first year, and there was little alternative. Evgenia went to stay at Kemsing in Kent with Arthur's mother who had written a warm and friendly letter welcoming her to the family. Ransome was still in Egypt over Christmas, and in February he went on to Sudan, where he stayed at Khartoum with the Governor-General. Finally he returned to England at the end of the month and they were able to start house hunting in the Lake District.

Although Evgenia gave up everything when she began living with Ransome, it has been suggested that life would not have been comfortable for her had she remained in Russia. She vehemently claimed to the end of her days that she was being watched by the KGB. Was it far-fetched imagining? Or perhaps the natural reaction of one who had been at the centre of the great events of 1917 and lived to see old age? Whatever the reason, those who knew the Ransomes in later life understood that the subject of Russia was taboo.

Throughout her life Evgenia remained loyal and supportive to Arthur, and she was always the positive one. Their letters tell us much about their relationship. For instance, when they came to leave the Lake District and move to East Anglia in 1935, Arthur had taken himself off in his new yacht, *Nancy Blackett*, leaving Evgenia to camp out in the barn and organise the packing:

> Our books (very noble of me to share the ownership, you must admit) are all packed and they terrify me by the amount of space they take. You know you haven't thrown away half the books you promised. You will have to do it at Levington. I won't let you off your promise; and in future for every new book you buy, or any way acquire and want to keep you will be made to throw out one of the old ones. You had better get accustomed to the idea before it is put into action. It will be less painful when the time comes to enforce the law.

For his part, Arthur could be scolding too. 'Got in by this morning's tide...I need hardly tell you, you lazy heartless creature that I found no letter at all.' More typical is this back-handed compliment about a photograph of Evgenia:

> There is a really lovely one of you. Anyone who did not know would think you were really lovely. Perfect profile and a smile that would melt Spitzbergen. The very gentlest, sweetest creature! I look an ass in all mine, so that's all right.

Chapter Five
SWALLOWS AND AMAZONS

As soon as Low Ludderburn had become their home in May 1925, Evgenia began to superintend the conversion of the old barn into a workroom. Ransome saw little of the builders, for he celebrated his return to the lake country with 'a perfect orgy' of fishing. The *Manchester Guardian* gave him a column in which to write a series of fishing essays, 'Rod and Line'. Eventually 150 weekly essays were published before the series ended in the autumn of 1929, by which time fishing with one eye on the following week's deadline had lost its appeal.

The cost of Low Ludderburn and its furnishings, the barn conversion and the purchase of the little car that they had promised themselves, came to a little over £1,000. To help meet the expense, *Racundra* was offered for sale at £300. The boat eventually changed hands for £220 to a young yachting writer, Adlard Coles. As part of the deal, which had been closed only after a series of misunderstandings and a flurried exchange of telegrams, the new owner had to agree to change the yacht's name. Coles sailed *Racundra* to England and wrote an account of the slow and laborious voyage in his book *Close Hauled*. Now that the yacht was safely anchored in an East Coast harbour, Coles offered to sell her back to Ransome for £350!

There were only a few months in which to enjoy the pleasures of Ludderburn before Ransome was sent to Russia. At Christmas the following year he was despatched to China to report on a revolution there. The newspaper articles he wrote following his visit to Hankow provided the material for *The Chinese Puzzle*, which was published in 1927. Years later he was to turn the experience to good use when he wrote *Missee Lee*, one of the most original of the Swallows and Amazons series.

By the spring of 1929 Ransome had grown tired of being at the *Manchester Guardian's* beck and call and was frustrated by the prospect of remaining a journalist for the remainder of his working life. In February the editor, C.P.Scott, had told him that he would like him to go to Moscow for a year or so. The crunch came the following month when Scott promised that he would make him the next literary editor at an 'enormous salary' if, in the meantime, he would become their correspondent in Berlin.

Ransome realised that the time had come to make a choice. He could either give up the idea of writing stories for children and go for a financially secure future at the cost of being tied to a desk in Manchester or rely on occasional reviews and essays — and whatever income his stories might bring. It was a fortnight before he went back to Scott and, with Evgenia's loyal support, gave three months notice. Almost immediately he began *Swallows and Amazons*.

Varying accounts survive of how *Swallows and Amazons* came to be written. This early version — found among Ransome's papers in the Brotherton Library archive at the University of Leeds — was drafted in the autumn of 1930.

About once in every five years a friend of mine who has an enormous family and lives in Syria brings his family home and spends the summer with them on the shores of a lake which he and his wife and I have known ever since we were ourselves children. We have played about in boats on it ever since we can remember...Anyhow this friend of mine, whom I will call Walker, looked forward always to coming home

Low Ludderburn. Just behind the wall stands the wooden garage that Ransome had built in order to house the little car he named Rattletrap. Beyond that is the converted barn in which he wrote Swallows and Amazons and five of its successors. The place is as quiet and peaceful as ever and still very much as the Ransomes knew it.

chiefly because of being able once more to sail in a small boat. Now about two years ago, when Mr Walker and all his children and his wife came home, he rushed off, as soon as they had unpacked, to a seaport town not far away and there bought two dinghies, one for himself and one for me, on the understanding that I was not to claim my one or indeed pay for it until he and his brood had gone back to their desert sands and camels and all the rest of that Eastern world. So for a whole summer, my dinghy, whose name *Swallow* was given her in memory of a long broken up *Swallow* in which we grown-ups had been young in our day, did not belong to me but was part of a regular fleet sailed by the Walkers. She proved to be the very best of little ships, and by the time the year was over, and boxes were being packed for the East, she was very much beloved by her owners, and I felt what a cruel thing it was that they should have to go off to their mullahs and mosques and leave me sailing in their dinghy in the great lake among the hills. It seemed most unfair.

And then, one day...I heard a motor car stop outside the gate of my cottage and, looking out under the big yew trees (for the cottage is several hundred years old), I saw a considerable crowd of people, mostly smallish, getting out of the motor car. I was as cross as two sticks, because though I had invited Mr Walker, the father of the family, I had warned him that for domestic reasons ONE would be enough, and that, on this occasion, he alone would be expected. He knew this well enough, and had it on his conscience, for instead of coming straight in, he lurked behind the gate. And then the gate opened and two of the Walkers, Titty (whose real name I never can remember) and Susan, came rushing in, each holding out an ENORMOUS scarlet leather Syrian slipper. Then came the others, and, shyly for him, Walker himself. And they all shouted 'Many Happy Returns'...the funny thing was that I had forgotten that it was my birthday. Well, there I was, feeling ashamed...They were leaving for Syria. They knew that henceforth I should be sailing the *Swallow* and instead of hating me, as well they might, they had brought me those slippers, which turned out to be as good as they were handsome and are my most comfortable slippers to this day. It was just then that I thought what fun it would be if I could write them a book about the *Swallow* and the lake and the island that was their playground, as it had been ours, and that of our parents before us.

That, I suppose, was really the beginning of the book. I said nothing about it to them, because I did not know whether I should ever be able to write it...

Apart from the use of a little literary embroidery, this account stands up to scrutiny and is confirmed by Ransome's working notes, his correspondence and his diary, as well as the diaries of Evgenia and Dora Altounyan. Towards the end of his life he claimed that the story was already written and that he had done a little name-changing to please the children. This assertion can be dismissed as the work of an author who was fearful that his own creative process was not receiving sufficient recognition.

'Mr Walker' was Ernest Altounyan, who was married to Dora Collingwood. Since 1919 they had been living in Aleppo, Syria, where Altounyan assisted his father in running the hospital. As a school friend of Robin Collingwood, Altounyan had also been invited to Lanehead, and was both a Lake District lover and a sailing enthusiast. His 'enormous family' consisted of Barbara 'Taqui' (born in 1917), Susie (1919), Mavis 'Titty' (1920), Roger (1922) and Brigit (1926). The family and their nurse visited England in 1928, and arrived at Windermere Station on 21st April. They were met by the Ransomes who drove the parents to their lodgings at Bank Ground Farm which lies between Lanehead (the Collingwood home) and the boathouses on the shore of Coniston Water. On 6th May, Altounyan went to Barrow and bought two sailing dinghies, one of which was delivered to the foot of the lake and put into the water. He arrived at Bank Ground around one o'clock the following morning, having sailed up the lake in the dark. Ransome continued his tale:

...a boat cannot do everything in a book. There must be people too, and of course the best possible people would be those very children who had sailed her and given me those slippers. And then I found other children coming in, and even the Walkers themselves doing, in my story, and saying, all sort of things that had not been planned for them. I began to understand that in writing about children one is writing about one's own childhood as well as theirs, and so, in a way, about childhood in general...before I knew what was happening, I was enjoying the writing of this book more than I have ever enjoyed writing any other book in my life. And I think I can put my finger on the thing which gave me the most pleasure. It was just this, the way in which the children in it have no firm dividing line between make-believe and reality, but slip in and out again and again, exactly as I had done when I was a child and as I rather fancy we all of us do in grown up life. Everything was possible, for me, just as it was for them, and yet there we all were with our feet hitting the earth quite firmly when we ran about. I and they slipped in and out of grown up 'native' life and in and out of the 'real' life of the explorers and pirates half a dozen times in a chapter. In a way we were making the best of both worlds. And I, at least, enjoyed myself like fun...

Swallows and Amazons began to take tangible form with the chapter headings, a very rough map and a list of the children and their ages. By 28th March 1929 he had written thirteen pages of the opening chapter, 'The Peak in Darien'. By the end of the month he had completed 45 pages which he brought in to the cottage and kept in a loose-leaf binder by his bedside at night. Molly Hamilton — the writer and politician whose friendship, he said, 'was like having an army at one's back'— encouraged him and introduced him to the publisher, Jonathan Cape, whom he had met two years before. Although the firm of Jonathan Cape had only been publishing since 1921 it had already gained a reputation for books which had individuality and style and its list included Ernest Hemingway, T.E. Lawrence and Hugh Lofting. With the promise of a contract, Ransome returned to his workroom and in 38 days completed the first draft, only taking time off occasionally to do a little fishing and to sail *Swallow* on Windermere. The diary charts his progress in loving detail, as Ransome — sometimes with as little as three pages in a day, sometimes with as many as fifteen —

tackled the chapters in chronological order.

But then, as the book did at last come to an end (though there was no reason why it should not have gone on for ever) I began to be very much afraid. For though the children in the book had taken things so much into their own hands that I could never be quite sure what they were to do or say next, there they were, labelled with the names of the Walkers. And oddly enough, I could not change their names, though it sounds so simple, just to go through the book with a pen and put new names in and cross out the old ones. As soon as I tried to change a name, there was a sort of revolt among the people in the book and nothing would go right. So there could be no possible pretending that the people in the book were not the people they actually were.

There is a clause about libel in agreements between authors and publishers, and when I looked it up I did not like the look of it. Besides that, the Walkers were among my best friends, and I began to wonder what would happen if they did not like their portraits, and still worse, if Captain John and Mate Susan, and Able-seaman Titty and the Boy Roger did not like theirs. And besides that there were the Amazons to think of, too...even if the people outside the book don't like the people inside the book, the people inside have got some sort of right to be alive. That's how I see them anyhow, and it's too late to alter them now. So I sent the book to the printer.

The Altounyan children —
Susie, Taqui, Titty (sitting) and
Roger.

And still I had not sent a word to Syria of what was going on in the old cottage under the yews. Out there they did not know that I had gone helter skelter. I dared not write. And I got more and more worried about what would happen when Mrs Walker, for example, read about her own children. I thought of tigresses defending their young. And yet, in a way, they were my children too, at least the ones in the book were, and the other ones outside the book had always counted me as a bit of their family.

After finishing the first draft of *Swallows and Amazons* Ransome began work on a new series of weekly articles for the *Manchester Guardian*. He seems to have been given a free hand by his great friend, Ted Scott, who had succeeded his father as editor. Such freedom had its drawbacks, for Ransome devoted upwards of three days each week to thinking of such subjects as 'John Peel', 'Speed and Travel', 'Dust', and 'These so-called Fairies' and delivering 1,800 words on each.

In September the Ransomes managed to spend a few days on holiday in Eire. The strain of meeting weekly deadlines had begun to effect his health, and it was a relief when the paper sent him to Egypt to cover the general election. Ransome's fitness always improved whilst at sea, and the voyage out gave him the opportunity to begin work on a revision of the Swallows story. A further bout of illness at Christmas while he was still in Egypt put a stop to journalism for a while and allowed the revision to continue. Finally, the book was finished in February 1930 after his return to England.

The original dedication of *Swallows and Amazons* was 'To the four for whom it was written in exchange for a pair of slippers.' The number was increased to six before publication, presumably to include the parents. The dedication was removed entirely in 1948, by which time he wanted to suppress all connection with the Altounyans. In the Author's Note which was written in 1958, but did not appear in the book until three years after his death in 1967, there is no reference to any children other than his brother, sisters and himself.

Having dispatched this script for publication, Ransome's letters show that he was indeed worried about the book's reception in Syria, but

Swallows and Amazons was most enthusiastically received, particularly by Ernest Altounyan, whose response showed that he had identified his family too closely with the characters in the story. 'You've made me to bulge with paternal pride, and I kept saying to myself as I read — damn fine sporting kids and then realising that they were mine!' Ransome was so pleased with their response to the book that he 'wanted to sit down right away and write another for them.'

Swallows and Amazons opens during the summer holidays of 1929 when John, Susan, Titty and Roger Walker receive a telegram from their father (a naval officer aboard ship at Malta) giving them permission to borrow a dinghy and sail off to camp on a nearby island. Their mother, their small sister Bridget and her nurse remain at Holly Howe farm where they have all been staying.

Nancy and Peggy Blackett live at Beckfoot, a house beside a small river flowing into the northern part of the lake. They sail in the *Amazon*, fly the skull and crossbones flag at her masthead and call themselves the Amazon Pirates. Their Uncle Jim is writing a book and lives with his parrot aboard a houseboat that is moored on the lake and is armed with a small cannon. His real name is James Turner, but when Titty sees him writing on deck with his green parrot beside him, she decides that he must be a retired pirate.

The Amazon pirates had camped on what they call Wild Cat Island long before the crew of the *Swallow* discover it. To regain their territory, they make a surprise attack on the Walker's camp and after a brief skirmish, they become allies with the Swallows against the houseboat man who is too busy to have time for them. They call him Captain Flint.

The allies plan a little private war, and during a night of high adventure on the lake, the houseboat is burgled. Able-seaman Titty has the good fortune to capture *Amazon* and is anchored off the rocky island where she overhears the thieves hide Captain Flint's old cabin trunk. He unjustly suspects the Swallows of the theft, but after Captain Nancy tips him the Black Spot, he handsomely apologises, and they make peace. Titty and Roger between them find the trunk which contains Captain Flint's old diaries and the book he had been writing. In gratitude he gives Titty his parrot, but not until he has been made to walk the plank for his misdemeanours. That night there is a thunderstorm, camping comes to an end, and the book closes as the allies part with a promise to meet again next year.

Reality and fiction come close together as the story opens. The Altounyan children and their nurse had spent some time at Bank Ground Farm by Coniston Water in the summer of 1928 after their parents had gone abroad on holiday. Originally Ransome called the farm in the story Bank Ground, only changing the name in the final revision to Holly Howe, which he borrowed from a house in Coniston village. The choice of the name Walker is surprising for it was the maiden name of Ivy, his first wife. He was writing in a 'Walker' loose-leaf binder, *Swallow* was looked after by a boatman called Walker, and John Walker was another well-known Bowness boatman.

The Peak in Darien, where the children picnic while waiting for the telegram, has been identified by a postcard of Friar's Crag at Keswick which

Ransome annotated. There are other possible candidates closer to the scene of the action which are worthy of consideration. Gale Naze Crag is a pine-crowned cliff which stands at the head of Windermere at the mouth of a deep bay similar to Holly Howe Bay. The strangely named promontary of High Peel Near beside Coniston Water has a fine view of Peel Island from its rocky eminence. Neither of these places is likely to have been available as a postcard to show to possible illustrators.

The eldest Walker is twelve-year-old Captain John. He is a serious-minded and responsible lad, destined to follow his father into the Royal Navy. Already his is an embryo naval officer and a trifle too self-confident and capable. Originally he was given the name Dick, perhaps because Ted Scott's son Dick was staying at Low Ludderburn for a time while Ransome was starting the story. Ten-year-old Mate Susan took Susie Altounyan's name and her place in the family. Here the connection ends, for the organised and motherly Susan looks after the other children rather as Evgenia looked after Arthur. This likeness was noticed by several of the young friends with whom they sailed in later years.

Able-seaman Titty was given Mavis Altounyan's unfortunate nickname which came from the story of Titty Mouse and Tatty Mouse that she had

The Holly Howe boathouse and the field climbing up to the farm is just as it appears in the opening of Swallows and Amazons.

loved when she was small. 'My Titty is a little eager imaginative child of about nine. No more,' wrote Ransome. She is the central character, and much of the book's freshness and innocence comes from her romantic vision which transforms ordinary everyday occurrences into something special. An avid reader, Titty has devoured all those books which Ransome himself had loved as a child. For Titty Altounyan, the name and superficial resemblance to the book's heroine became a burden:

He took my name and if it had been an ordinary one I could have pretended it was another Mary or Joan and shrugged it off. But it was my own special nickname and a rather silly one at that. To hammer home the damage, he took some of my characteristics I suppose, but it wasn't and it couldn't be me. So at a time when I was struggling to come to terms with the world, at twelve years old, when I came to England to school, at an age when, unless you've been brought up by Fagin, honesty is so important, I felt a complete hoax. But I was too polite to tell him so. I loved Uncle Arthur and Aunt Genia. They were nice, kind, exciting and interesting people and I never stopped loving them.

The irrepressible Boy Roger, 'aged seven and no

The pine-topped promontory of Gale Naze Crag at the head of Windermere is a strong candidate for the origin of Darien.

longer the youngest in the family', whom the Altounyans thought 'very true to life', provides a foil to his more earnest siblings and enabled Ransome to introduce some quiet humour. Bridget Walker took her name from Brigit Altounyan, but as Ransome noted on his list of characters, she did not matter as she was too young to be a member of the *Swallow's* crew.

In Greek mythology the Amazons were a race of female warriors who destroyed their right breast so as not to interfere with their use of a bow. In more recent times, some of the young women who took up arms during the Russian Revolution were known as Amazons. Ransome confided that Evgenia and her sister Iraida 'prefer pistols to powder puffs and swords to parasols'. Iraida had once commanded 300 'wildly devoted sailormen'. Were they the original Amazons?

In his *Autobiography* Ransome says that the Amazons 'sprung to life one day when I was sailing on Coniston and saw two little girls playing on the lake-shore'. There were only a few children to be seen on the margin of the lake in the 1920s, according to Pauline Marshall who spent her childhood next door to Bank Ground Farm at Bank Ground Cottage. She claims that the girls on the shore were her elder sister, Georgie, and herself. Taqui, the eldest of the Altounyan children who wrote lively letters to her Uncle Arthur in the Nancy manner, may have contributed to the character. However, Captain Nancy Blackett is such a remarkable young lady that she owes little to any 'original'.

Suzanna Hamilton as Susan and Stephen Grendon as Roger camping on Peel Island in a scene from Claude Whatham's 1974 film of Swallows and Amazons.

At first, the elder Amazon, aged 13, was to be called Jane Walker, aged 13, while her sister Mary, whose proper name was Ruth, was a year younger. They had a three-year-old brother, Tom. Eventually Ransome decided to give the name Walker to the Swallows, and the Amazons became Nancy, Peggy and Tom Smith before he finally changed their names to Nancy (Ruth) and Peggy (Margaret) Blackett. Peggy's name was the same as that of Ted Scott's daughter, who had been christened Margaret, but because she disliked the name she was always known as Peggy. Ransome's papers have failed to reveal anyone called Nancy, but Ruth was Robin Collingwood's daughter, and in all probability the name was chosen in order that Ransome could claim that the Amazons were 'ruthless'.

In essentials, Wild Cat Island is Peel Island on Coniston Water, although there are features from three islands. The hidden harbour, look-out point and the island's rocky cliffs are all from Peel Island; the landing place and the tall pine tree are likely to have been taken from Blake Holme, close to the shores of Windermere, and there is a grand place for a camp among the trees of Ramp Holme south of the Windermere ferry.

The description of the crowded Rio Bay and the islands offshore is so exactly like Bowness-on-Windermere that Ransome freely admitted the connection in a publisher's biographical note:

He thinks he has let out rather too many secrets in his books, and when people pester him to tell them things that he has carefully left untold, he has only one answer: 'The ONLY way to keep a secret is NEVER to answer questions'.

The name of the lake? Here he admits that the Rio of the books is Bowness-on-Windermere. But certain things are borrowed from Coniston, and the geography has been carefully mixed, so as to keep at least a few places secret. Everything described in the

books is to be found, but not always as near to or far from other things as it is shown on the map.

The lake itself is remarkably like Windermere. During the Swallows' voyage to the island they make a point of not noticing other lake vessels, although Ransome makes it clear that the lake is far from the deserted ocean of the explorers' imagination. Once they have become established on the island the steamer service has some significance for them when they watch for 'Roger's bedtime' steamer. At that time there were three passenger steamers sailing on Windermere and operated by the LMS Railway Company: *Cygnet*, *Tern* and *Swift*. The *Cygnet* was broken up in 1970 but the *Swift* was still in service until 1980. The pride of the 'steamer' fleet today is the *Tern* which has been in service since 1891. During the Second World War the vessel was commandeered by the Admiralty and served as a naval patrol boat on the lake. She has been restored to her original appearance with a replica of the tall smoke-stack and saloons which have a touch of Victorian luxury.

Her unusual canoe-shaped bow serves to identify her as the steamer sailing out of Rio Bay in the illustration by Clifford Webb for *Swallows and Amazons*.

The man on the houseboat is a remarkably honest self-portrait, for the irritable and hasty-tempered Flint, like his creator, is large and bald — only the soup-strainer moustache is missing. The houseboat resembles the steam yacht *Esperance*, which was built in 1869 for a successful industrialist, H.W. Schneider. He had recently acquired the Belsfield, a large house overlooking Bowness Bay, and needed the vessel to take him on his daily journey to and from Lakeside Station where his private train took him to his ironworks in Barrow. Breakfast was served in the luxurious cabin by the butler while the steam yacht glided down the lake in near silence. Ransome confessed to Oliver Scott, whose family had owned the yacht and used it as a houseboat in the 1930s, that he had once sailed *Swallow* alongside and stood up in the boat so that he could peep into the cabin. *Esperance* is on view at the Windermere

(Opposite)
The beautifully restored 'steamer'
Tern *which appears in one of Clifford Webb's illustrations for* **Swallows and Amazons.** *is a surviving link with the days when Arthur was at school in Windermere.*

(Above)
Esperance *has had her engine removed and lies alongside the jetty at the Windermere Steamboat Museum. Her powerful rakish bow was designed to break a path through any thin ice she might encounter on her daily journeys to and from the foot of the lake.*

(Right)
To complete the illusion a small brass cannon on the foredeck and a cabin table laid out with a feast and presided over by a green parrot greet the many enthusiasts who visit the museum each year.

Steamboat Museum where she has been joined by the Altounyan's dinghy *Mavis* in which they had learned to sail in 1928. Because of the part she had played in the inspiration of *Swallows and Amazons* she was renamed *Amazon* at a ceremony to mark the inauguration of the Arthur Ransome Society in 1990. Some say that the *Gondola*, which is still carrying passengers on Coniston Water, was the model for the houseboat, but apart from its greater resemblance to Ransome's illustrations, support for *Esperance* can be found in his reaction to the television dramatisation of *Swallows and Amazons* made by Films of Windsor Ltd for the BBC in 1962. Though hardly anything that the film-makers did escaped Ransome's criticism, their use of *Esperance* passed unchallenged.

The Amazon River can be identified as the River Crake which he had known so well as a boy. It flows out of the south end of Coniston Water into the waterlily-covered Allan Tarn, which was renamed Octopus Lagoon.

Beckfoot, the Amazon's home, is a substantial grey-stone house with a stable block and a lawn leading down to the river. Numerous enthusiasts have searched for Beckfoot without a consensus settling on a particular building. One possibility can be found just across the water from Peel Island where Oxen House lies close to the mouth of Torver Beck. There is a fine, conspicuous boat-house, but the Victorian gabled building itself is not the least like Beckfoot. Towards the head of Coniston Water, Lanehead and the neighbouring Tent Lodge each have their supporters. Close to Fell Foot Park at the southern end of Windermere, Town Head possesses many of the features of Ransome's drawings. There are a number of private references and jokes in the story and the reversal of Town Head and Beckfoot would be in keeping, for he enjoyed playing with words.

Ransome gave away the secret that the Cormorant Island was based on the island of Silver Holme on Windermere. However, he referred the director of the television dramatisation to the tiny islet about a hundred metres south of Peel Island:

> At least half the best details are not to be found on Windermere. It is really important that they get the

harbour right, and I can take them straight to the very photogenic Holly Howe, the harbour on the island etc. Not one of the islands on Windermere offers such chances. Also the little rocky island where they recovered Uncle Jim's box is on Coniston... 'the lake' combines both Windermere and Coniston. In order to give the right picture, I think he [the director] will have to find some ingenious method of using the populous Bowness Bay and the (comparatively) steeply wooded shores of Coniston.

Ten years later, Claude Whatham achieved just such a successful amalgamation when he used most of the original places in the excellent feature film of *Swallows and Amazons*, made in 1973.

Ransome experimented with different versions of the final chapters of the book. In one of the accounts Titty and Roger are allowed to go to Cormorant Island to look for treasure and in doing so miss the arrival of the Amazons. Having found the box, which they cannot move, Titty leaves Roger sitting on the treasure and returns to the island for help:

> She took *Swallow* into the harbour because it was nearer than the landing place. She found the beach strewn with the gear Peggy had thrown out of *Amazon* when Nancy had taken *Amazon* to row to Houseboat Bay to tip Captain Flint the Black Spot.
>
> 'They've come,' she said to herself. 'And we were so busy looking for the treasure that we never saw them.'
>
> She ran along the path to the camp. Just before she got there she stopped short. There were Captain Nancy, Mate Peggy, Mate Susan and Captain John. That was all right. But in the middle of them was a man, a large man with a bald head, sitting on the ground and drinking tea out of a mug, It was Captain Flint himself and Susan was handing him a lump of cake.
>
> For a moment Titty thought of hiding until he had gone. She slipped back behind a tree. But it was too late Nancy had seen her.
>
> 'Here she is,' she cried. 'Come along Able-seaman. There's no need to lurk. He's friendly at the moment.'

Ransome was adamant that he had written *Swallows and Amazons* and its successors to please

(Above)
***The hidden harbour on Peel Island — the
Mecca for Swallows and Amazons enthusiasts.***
(Ted Alexander)

(Right)
***'What a place,' said the able-seaman. 'I expect
somebody hid on the island hundreds of years
ago and kept his boat here.'***

himself: 'He holds strong views on the cataloguing of children's books by age-groups, and when asked for readers of what age his own books are designed, replies, "Between forty six and sixty four."' To his publisher he confessed that there was an age-group that he did not write for. When Jonathan Cape quoted a favourable review which referred to 'teenage boys and girls' in an advertisement for *Peter Duck*, Ransome wrote asking for the mention of teenagers to be withdrawn. 'I do not write for those wretched teens except by accident…The teens are an unsatisfactory accidental public.'

In spite of Ransome's assertion that 'Good

books are not written for anyone. They are over-heard '— a statement which partly concealed his art — he had a specific audience in mind. He maintained that his 'most useful' readers were those aged between seven and thirteen, which is exactly the age range of his Swallows and Amazons in the first of the series. Indeed, to him, it was important to have a character within a couple of years of the age of potential readers with whom they could identify. A spread of ages would enable readers to identify with older characters as they themselves grew up. He considered that he would be assisting readers by omitting almost all references to appearance. Later in the series, he tells us that Dorothea has straw-coloured plaits and Dick wears spectacles, but the mention in the *Swallows and Amazons* draft of Nancy and Peggy's dark curly hair was removed.

It was probably Stephen Spurrier's interpretation of the children, as much as the author's predilection for accuracy, that made Ransome reject the illustrations commissioned for *Swallows and Amazons*. Although Spurrier was a fine artist and his drawings are superb, he focussed attention on the children, who are invariably shown facing the reader. Only Spurrier's spirited endpaper map that doubled as a dust jacket in the first edition,

and his map of Wild Cat Island were to appear in print. These were retained until 1970 when, on Evgenia's insistence, they were replaced by rather bland substitutes which fail to capture the spirit of the book.

When Clifford Webb was asked to produce drawings for the second edition of the book in 1931, Ransome told him that the youngsters should be portrayed so 'any child can identify with any character'. The artist was to devote all his energy to creating a romantic landscape that 'no child can invent'. For this reason, Ransome favoured back views, and the only drawing of Webb's that he rejected was a full face portrayal of Titty. The only other stipulation that Ransome laid down was that the height of the children should be in proportion to each other. When he finally came to illustrate the books himself, Ransome's own drawings of children were practically anonymous, leaving almost everything to the imagination. His intention was to allow the reader to view the action by 'looking over the shoulder' whenever possible, and this device works remarkably well in a number of his illustrations.

Shortly before *Swallows and Amazons* was published the first review appeared in the *Manchester Guardian*. It was written by Malcolm

Muggeridge, who had been recommended to the staff of the newspaper by Ransome the previous year. He made a number of discerning observations:

> Mr Ransome has the same magical power that Lewis Carroll had of being a child in terms of himself. He never talks down: never finds it necessary to be patronising or sentimental...the explorers in *Swallows and Amazons* are supplied by a farmer only thinly disguised as one of the less hostile natives, and buy their lemonade over the counter — a fact which does not at all prevent it from becoming vitriolic grog. That is to say, the book is the very stuff of play.

One of the few reviews to offer any criticism

(Opposite)
Townhead, near Fell Foot Park at the southern end of Windermere, has the look of Beckfoot, but there are several other possible places.

(Above)
Ransome's drawing of Beckfoot for Swallowdale.

(Below)
The 'little rocky island' on Coniston Water that the Altounyan children called Cormorant Island was also the place that Ransome told the film-makers to use.

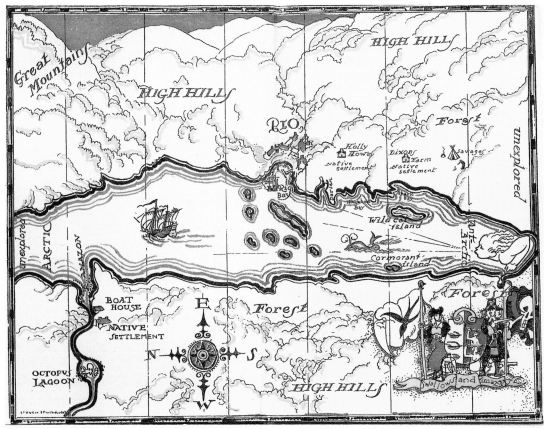

(Opposite, top)
Bank Ground Farm, the inspiration for Holly Howe, with Coniston Water and Gondola in the distance.

(Lower)
Lazy Bay on Windermere is surrounded by trees and difficult to identify from the water, making it a very good Horseshoe Cove.

(This page, top)
Stephen Spurrier's endpaper map for Swallows ans Amazons.

(Right)
Cormorant Island is generally held to be Silver Holme on Windermere. Once the cormorants left the island, the trees had a chance to regenerate. The birds now roost on one of the islands north of Bowness Bay, and already appear to have killed the tree on which they perch.

Captain John (Simon West) entering harbour using the leading lights for the first time in one of the beautifully observed scenes in the Swallows and Amazons *film.*

was by an anonymous writer for the *Yorkshire Post* who thought it: 'A most delectable book, written with a little too much detail, a trifle too consciously for sailors and their progeny, nurtured from birth on seafaring terms...' — a view shared by many of those who have failed to come under its spell.

Molly Hamilton, Ransome's staunch friend who had been so encouraging at the start, wrote two glowing reviews, the second for Jonathan Cape's house journal, *Now and Then*:

They are real, from the very first moment when we meet Roger 'tacking' up the field, through all their adventures (including that really marvellous piece of imaginative penetration called 'Titty Alone') right up to the grand carouse of the close. Real themselves, they bring their world with them — a world of intense, absorbed seriousness, in which the boundaries between the real and the imagined grow thin, and wonder spreads over both. This is indeed Mr Ransome's miracle — that without one extraneous or self-conscious word he has cast this

mysterious and lovely glow over his lake...

There were a couple of acute miss-readings: an anonymous writer for the Scotsman thought the whole thing was a fantasy made up by the children whilst remaining in their garden at home, and Barbara Euphan Todd told readers of the *Spectator* that the story took place among the creeks of Chichester Harbour!

Ransome was particularly pleased with the review by Sylvia Lynd, to whom, years earlier, he had proposed marriage:

John is the eldest by a year or two, anything from twelve to fourteen years old — young, but not incredibly young — to sail a boat on his own responsibility. His sister Susan is old enough to cut bread and butter, and is best at buttered eggs, though, as the farmer's wife points out, most people are best at boiled ones. Titty, the next one, is young enough to enjoy playing imaginative games on her own account, Roger is young enough not to be able to swim and to like running messages.

With such favourable reviews, it is not surprising that Jonathan Cape told him to forget about the proposed book of essays and hurry up and write another.

Chapter Six
THE HIDDEN VALLEY

On the day that *Swallows and Amazons* was published, Ransome was consulting a specialist in London. He had been unwell for some time and the doctor diagnosed a stomach ulcer, recommending that he should stay in bed on a diet of bismuth, olive oil and milk and give up smoking. The treatment appeared to be successful so that by mid-September he felt he would be able to turn his attention to writing again. With Cape so insistent that he should begin another Swallows and Amazons story, Ransome put aside the successor to *Old Peter's Russian Tales* that he had been planning, but, before he could begin, his ulcer flared up again and he decided to seek a second opinion. Dr Forest Smith warned him against eating or drinking anything which had been cooked in aluminium. His advice was to continue with the milk diet and eat more in order to put on weight. Soon afterwards Ransome wrote the opening scene of *Peter Duck*, and then abandoned it in favour of a more obvious sequel to *Swallows and Amazons*.

In January 1931 he started work on 'The Shipwrecked Swallows' or 'The Camp in Swallowdale'. A week later, after he had completed 55 pages, he wrote to Ernestine Evans at Lippincott, the American publisher of *Swallows and Amazons*:

My life won't be worth living over here unless the next book does what all the children I know assume it's going to do, namely, tell what else happens to the Swallows and the Amazons when they meet again next year. That is taken for granted and I am told, in every tone of authority, what NOT TO LEAVE OUT....Between ourselves and very very private. It begins right off with a shipwreck, thus letting me get

rid of the boat temporarily, and the subsequent book describes what happens to the ship-wrecked Swallows in their camp in the hills above the western shore of the lake. Enough of seafaring. Here are land adventures, how they live and what they do during the time when, while Swallow is being repaired, they are really and truly forced to do the best they can on land. It seems to be generally assumed that there jolly well ought to be a shipwreck. So I've provided a really good shipwreck and the rest of the book follows on naturally. After all, folk have to live, even when wrecked on the mainland.

While Ransome was living at Low Ludderburn, he used to to try out his stories on his neighbour's children, Desmond and Richard Kelsall, who lived less than a mile across the valley at Barkbooth. Colonel Kelsall, their father, was a great fishing enthusiast, and the two men frequently went fishing together. The boys sometimes visited the workroom in the Ludderburn barn to listen to the latest episode of whatever book was being written at the time, while Evgenia prepared a feast. Desmond delighted Ransome by anticipating the opening of *Swallowdale* when he said that he thought John was too good and in the next book he should become over-confident and wreck *Swallow*. When signatures were needed for the Ship's Papers, the boys obliged by signing 'John Walker' and 'Roger'. The claw print of a parrot was also required, and they arranged for their own parrot to leave a sooty mark when it perched on a piece of paper that they had wrapped round a broom handle.

The book progressed steadily throughout January. There is a string of confident entries in Ransome's diary for that month: 'Wild Cat Island'

(Opposite, top) *The lower reaches of the River Amazon were based on the River Crake which flows from the foot of Coniston Water. The reeds in which the Amazons hid during the war in Swallows and Amazons are clearly seen.*

(Lower) *Trout Tarn is easily identified from the sketch map that Ransome drew of the area. Its inspiration was Beacon Tarn, one of the most beautiful of the lower Lake District tarns. Beyond the northern ridge the distant peaks of Dow Crag and Coniston Old Man dominate this view. The easiest approach to the tarn is along the lane from Water Yeat near the foot of Coniston Water.*

(This page, top left) *Between the main road and Beacon Tarn lie the two waterfalls and a hidden valley that appear to have inspired the secret valley of Swallowdale. Apart from its close conformity to the text, the lower waterfall resembles the illustration by Clifford Webb.*

(Lower left) *During the summer the upper falls are more than half-hidden by the bracken and are easily missed, but in winter they can be readily seen in the fellside less than 100 yards above the lower falls — just as it says in the text.*

(Below) *John and Susan were introduced to fly-fishing at Trout Tarn. The flies that had been tied for them by Captain Flint were woodcock and orange and black spider (top) and dark snipe and purple (bottom left). (Bottom right) The coch-y-bonddhu fly after which the Renolds' dinghy was named.*

Jonathan Cape (right) and his partner
G. Wren Howard in the late 1920s.

12pp.. 'Secret Valley' 6pp...'Shipwreck' 14pp...'No
Ship' 11pp... 'Cast Ashore' 11pp...'Camp in Cove'
10pp...'A.B. in Command' 13pp...'Swallowdale'
11pp.' At this point, after he had completed 81
pages, he made a careful list of the contents.

When *Swallowdale* was published, Ransome
thought it necessary to write an introduction for
the benefit of those who had not read *Swallows
and Amazons*. After giving an outline of the events
in the first book, he continues:

> Afterwards of course, the Swallows had to go south
> to school, but in the Christmas holidays Captain
> Flint chartered a wherry on the Norfolk Broads and
> they all spent a week in it with him, Amazons and
> Swallows together, planning what they would do
> next summer, and making up a story about an old
> sailor and a voyage to the Caribbees.

Now the summer holidays had come round again.
The Swallows had again come north to Holly Howe,
looking forward to more adventures with Captain
Flint and the Amazons. But the Amazons had not
come to Holly Howe to meet them; and this book
opens with Captain John, Mate Susan, Able-seaman
Titty, Boy Roger and the parrot setting out once
more for Wild Cat Island, expecting to find that
Nancy and Peggy are waiting for them there, or, perhaps, in the houseboat with Captain Flint.

In the story, the Amazons have an impossibly
strict Great Aunt staying at Beckfoot and they are
only free to join their allies from time to time.
After John has run *Swallow* on to a rock and they
have swum ashore, the shipwrecked mariners
camp in a secret valley in the fells which they call
Swallowdale. Sailing has been brought to an end
until the Rio boatbuilder can repair the *Swallow*,
but that is not the end of the action. The Amazons
make a surprise attack and, a few days later, deliver
a message by an arrow fired in secret from under

the nose of the Great Aunt. Their message sends the Swallows trekking across the moor to the River Amazon and an overnight camp half way up the mountain. The following day the Great Aunt departs and, reunited again, the Swallows and Amazons climb to the summit. After this successful expedition, Susan and John take a passage aboard *Amazon*, but Titty and Roger try to return across the moor and become lost in the fog. Roger twists his ankle and has to spend the night with a charcoal burner. The story ends after *Swallow* has been repaired and the Swallows and Amazons return to Wild Cat Island.

Once Ransome had a clear outline, he wrote another 12 pages on 'Life in Swallowdale' and followed this with 12 pages he called 'Green Feather'. The first draft was completed by the middle of May, without chapters XVI to XIX. The Amazon's surprise attack was added later, and Titty's memorable exercise in witchcraft was not completed until after the final chapter. Writing *Swallowdale* was not quite the effortless undertaking that *Swallows and Amazons* had been, but it was nothing like the struggle Ransome endured over some of the later books.

In March 1931 he sent his daughter a copy of *Swallows and Amazons*. Tabitha was almost 21, so it is not altogether surprising that the book did not have the appeal for her that it might have done ten years earlier. In her *Reminiscences* Tabitha recalled that her mother sometimes drafted her letters to Arthur. She responded to the gift by saying that the book was 'churned out and tired', and that she had been unable to finish it. Tabitha was still capable of wounding her father and her verdict upset and depressed him. Although Ransome rarely met his daughter, he always remembered her at Christmas and on her birthday. To mark her 21st birthday, he wrote a long and heavy-handed letter advising her on the importance of living within her income and how she should approach marriage. After letting himself go for eight pages he concluded: 'Writing this, I somehow forget your letters and remember a round woolly Babba of long ago...'

Both parties made attempts at a reconciliation, but it was too late; by then the hurts had become too deep. Although he had agreed that Ivy should keep his library when they were divorced, the books had become a bone of contention and featured regularly in correspondence with Ivy. Inevitably Tabitha had become involved, and in 1929 she wrote to tell him that the books were all that she had ever got out of having a father. Ransome's letters to his first wife invariably had a bitter tone which was missing from those of Ivy:

> Wednesday August 21st 1931
> Dear Arthur
>   Thank you for the cheque £21.16.8. Being as you say, my allowance at the rate of £100 P.A. I don't think I can describe the relief. It has been awful all this while, and I have been frightened.
>   Ivy

Under the terms of the divorce, Ivy received a third of his income, and this additional expenditure added to his worries. *Swallows and Amazons* was selling slowly, and as his savings dwindled it became imperative that *Swallowdale* should succeed.

After a thorough revision, which included writing a new opening chapter, the book was finished by the end of July. It was longer than his publisher wanted, but G. Wren Howard, Jonathan Cape's partner, liked the story and thought it better than *Swallows and Amazons*. So *Swallowdale* was published without further revision.

What sort of a person was Wren Howard who took on the responsibility of looking after Ransome and was immensely patient and encouraging throughout their long association? Wren Howard was ten years younger than Ransome, and after Cambridge University and a distinguished military career in the First World War he began to develop his own ideas about book design and production. It was Wren Howard who gave Cape books their distictive style, insisting on using good quality paper, boards and binding cloth. His sense of design is evident in the Swallows and Amazons books which had the indefinable look and feel of quality — particularly before the restrictions imposed during the Second World War.

Swallowdale is a richer book than the plot might suggest, largely due to its underlying theme of the Swallows' introduction to the lake country of Ransome's youth, with strong autobiographical links to his own childhood holidays at Swainsons

(This page, top) *Horseshoe Cove. 'Swallow...was slipping across the smooth water of the sheltered cove towards a beach of white shingle below thick green trees.'*

(Left) *The valley which apparently inspired Swallowdale lies between a fine knickerbocker-breaker and the rocks which provide a vantage point similar to the Watch Tower Rock.*

(Opposite, top) *Because of the popularity of the climb to the summit of Coniston Old Man (Kanchenjunga) the path has become badly eroded in recent years.*

(Lower) *The path down which Nancy led the Swallows leads to the surprisingly blue water of Low Water Tarn.*

Farm at Nibthwaite. As if to underline the association, the farm where the shipwrecked Swallows collect milk and supplies is given the same name. As a boy, Ransome slid down a sloping rock he called the Knickerbockerbreaker, and from time to time his trousers had to be darned by Annie Swainson. In *Swallowdale* Roger slides down the steep slope into the valley and is darned by Mary Swainson. While they are unable to sail on the lake, the Swallows learn to fish for trout, go boating down the River Crake and climb Coniston Old Man — just as Arthur had done as a boy. This traditional way of life was already well into decline when he began writing and, for the most part, vanished for ever with the outbreak of the Second World War. Ransome may have been a little vague about the locations he wished to conceal, but he was meticulous in the accuracy he gave to local colour.

As members of a well-known local family, the Amazons are established within an intimate rural society to which the land-bound Swallows are

temporarily admitted. Roger, in particular, gains from this experience and spends the night in a charcoal burner's hut, where he eats a duck's egg and learns about the Grasmere Sports. He also joins Neddy Swainson singing hunting songs while John is busy working on Swallow's new mast. Ransome quotes ' Sandys' Hunting Song' that he probably heard in the Hark to Melody at Bigland as a young man. Myles Sandys lived at Graythwaite Hall, ten miles north of Ulverston. The song describes a legendary hunt which took place in 1743.

> Of such a fox chase there niver was known,
> The huntsmen and followers were instantly thrown.
> To keep within sound didn't lie in their power,
> For hounds chased the fox eighty mile in five hour.

Considering the rough fell country over which the hunt travelled, however, it is likely that 'eighty' is a corruption of eighteen. In Ransome's version of the song the word 'thrown' is used instead of the dialect 'thrawn', meaning exhausted.

The artist Clifford Webb was commissioned to illustrate both *Swallowdale* and the new edition of *Swallows and Amazons*. Webb spent several days at Low Ludderburn in April and sketched the *Swallow* as Ransome sailed to and fro on the lake. He took Webb across Coniston Water to Peel Island and then to the foot of the lake. He was outwardly polite about the illustrations. 'The night scene in the Amazon River. Magnificent. And the fishing scene with Roger attached to the pike. And I very much like the one with the lot of them pushing off the boat laden with wood.' Privately he was scathing. 'Webb. Damned ASS.'

Webb's drawings may not altogether have pleased Ransome, but they succeed admirably in conveying the romantic feeling of the Lake District landscape that he sought. Many of them depict places that are easily recognisable and so make excellent starting points for readers seeking to uncover Ransome's secrets. Above all, they provide a guide to the real identity of the secret valley

Miterdale has a beautiful valley head half-circled by the crags, but is it Swallowdale? Who knows? (David Sewart)

of Swallowdale.

Ransome prepared a rough map which shows that the valley is situated at the foot of Beacon Hill and near to Trout Tarn. Beacon Fell is situated to the west of Coniston Water and near the foot of the lake. Beacon Tarn lies in a nearby hollow and is clearly the inspiration for Trout Tarn. Webb drew Trout Tarn, the valley of Swallowdale and its two waterfalls. Using the illustrations as a guide, the waterfalls can be found between Beacon Fell and the road which runs along the western side of the lake. The beck plunges down the lower falls and flows through bracken-covered fellside to enter the lake in a bay which looks very like Webb's drawing of Horseshoe Cove.

The best way to discover the waterfall is to find the beck where it flows through a conduit under the road and to follow it across some marshy ground. By keeping close to the beck, the lower waterfall can be heard above, except during periods of draught, and then it is a simple matter of being guided by the sound of the water. Having climbed up beside the falls, the explorer enters a small hidden valley through which the beck runs. Nearby is a fine Watch Tower Rock with views towards Coniston Water and Peel Island. The area

The Swallows and Amazons saw wild goats on the summit of Kanchenjunga. Nowadays the goats have been replaced by very friendly sheep.

is marked on the map as Long Scars. There is plenty in the text of *Swallowdale* to aid identification: 'Above them the waterfall poured down noisily from ledge to ledge of rock, and they could go no further without climbing up the rocks beside the falling water or getting out of the long winding gully that the stream had carved for itself in the moor...shut in by another waterfall at the head of it not a hundred yards away...' Peter Duck's cave was simply borrowed from the dozens to be found in the old copper mining district among the Coniston fells to the north.

Even though there can be little doubt that the waterfalls are right enough, is the little valley the inspiration for the secret valley that has so captured the imagination of his readers? Again, the text is explicit: 'slopes of rock and heather that rose so steeply that when the explorers looked up they could see nothing but the sky above them...They climbed opposite sides of the valley

(Above)
Traditional charcoal burning, after a painting by A. Heaton Cooper.

(Left)
The waterfall past which the Swallows climbed on the way to their half-way camp was also the scene of the youthful Ransome's encounter with W. G. Collingwood in Coppermines Valley.

and looked back at each other. They found that they had only to go a few yards from the edge of it not to see that it was there...They scrambled down again to meet at the bottom...From this upper end of the valley...its steep sides, one of them, on the right, almost a precipice of rock, with heather growing in the cracks of it, and the other, on the left, not so steep, with grass on it, bracken and loose stones...She went a few yards further on along the edge of it and then came down by a sheep track...'

The valley fits all these descriptions, but is not at all like Ransome's drawing which replaced Webb's when he re-illustrated the book in 1938. There are many within the Arthur Ransome Society who have rejected Webb's illustration in favour of Ransome's and believe that he had the head of Miterdale in mind. Miterdale is one of the most impressive secret valleys of the Lake District, stretching for five miles from the village of Eskdale Green to Burnmoor. The dalehead itself is a semi-circle of crags and waterfalls enclosing a flat area through which the River Mite flows placidly down the valley. It is a gem of a place — a much larger version of Ransome's drawing, tucked away in the middle of the fells and remote from civilisation. Unlike other places which are associated with the Swallows and Amazons books, there is no means of knowing whether Ransome was aware of Miterdale's existence or ever visited the dalehead. Perhaps Swallowdale is a blend of Long Scars and Miterdale and the key to Ransome's closely guarded secrets lies in his practice in the early stories of combining various people and places in order to conceal their identity. Should his oft repeated 'All the places can be found...' be interpreted as 'Some of the places are a mixture, the components of which can be found...'?

Another confusing location is Horseshoe Cove, the scene of *Swallow's* shipwreck. One of Webb's representations of the cove resembles Lazy Bay, south of Rawlinson's Nab on Windermere, and this is supported by the text. The other looks more like the bay where the Long Scars beck enters Coniston Water.

Kanchenjunga, as Ransome freely admitted, is Coniston Old Man, a mountain which had a special fascination for him. He was taken up as a baby, and whenever he was abroad, he carried a lucky

A preserved charcoal burners' hut in Grizedale Forest.

stone from the summit as a talisman. In later years, when he was yearning to return to the lake country, he longed to 'crawl' up the Old Man. From the summit all the mountain tops that Nancy pointed out to the Swallows can be seen, but only those who are extremely fortunate with the weather will be able to catch a glimpse of the Isle of Man.

Before settling on the name Kanchenjunga, Ransome had considered calling the mountain Everest or Popocatepetl. Apart from its very appealing name, Kanchenjunga was in the public eye at around the time *Swallowdale* was being written because of the expeditions that were unsuccessfully attempting to conquer it, and photographs and articles were appearing in the *Manchester Guardian* and *The Times*.

The Swallows trek across High Moor, which is similar to Little Arrow Moor below Coniston Old Man, the scene of the first sighting of a flying saucer. The four firs which guide the Swallows on their way grew in, of all places, the Lanehead garden.

***Cumberland and Westmorland wrestling at the
Grasmere Sports.***

(Ed Geddard)

Beyond the lagoon which the Swallows discovered in *Swallows and Amazons*, the Amazon River
resembles Yewdale Beck to the north of Coniston
village. It flows placidly through the meadows,
close to where Ransome camped as a young man,
before passing under Yewdale Bridge and becoming a rocky mountain stream. To complete the
association, the bridge over the River Amazon is
called Udal Bridge. The description of the
Swallows' Half-way Camp and the mountaineers'
dash to the summit the following morning, sug-

gests that the camp is situated beside the Low
Water Beck, some distance beyond the
Coppermines Youth Hostel.

The names of real rocks were used for the haz-
ards that the returning climbers have to avoid
while drifting through Rio Bay in the fog. The
Hen and Chicken rocks are to be found south of
the Windermere Ferry. There are at least two real
Heald Woods in the southern part of the Lake
District, although neither is to be found where it
appears in the story: one is situated beside
Windermere and the other to the east of Coniston
Water.

Among the local characters that appear in both
Swallows and Amazons and *Swallowdale*, the charcoal burners, known as the Billies, have a special

appeal. Ransome had a good ear for lakeland dialect, and when someone at Cape questioned the accuracy of Old Billy's observation, 'Folk generally what do,' he retorted: 'This is exactly as it should be. It is good lake country speech, and the speaker would have choked if he had been asked to say it otherwise.' In fact, Ransome's reproduction of the local vernacular is an essential feature of his picture of the area in the early years of the 20th century. He sympathetically depicts the charcoal burners who, like the old couple at Swainson's Farm and the Broadsmen Harry Bangate and Jim Woodall in *The Big Six*, represent a way of life threatened by progress.

Charcoal burning in the woods of Furness can be traced back to mediaeval times, when large amounts of charcoal were needed to fire the nearby iron ore bloomeries. Considerable quantities of timber were required as one ton of charcoal resulted from burning five tons of timber and, depending on the size of the mound, the actual burn took between three and five days.

Hazel was widely used for making charcoal and a continuous supply was ensured by means of coppicing. Trees were cut down almost to ground level and from around the base as many as twenty new shoots would appear. Regeneration was ensured every fifteen years or so when the shoots were cut in the autumn. The Beckfoot Coppice was almost certainly an old hazel coppice of this sort. Charcoal made from ash wood was used in the making of gunpowder until the introduction of new explosives brought production to an end after the First World War.

As a boy Ransome made friends with the charcoal burners working in the woods near Nibthwaite. When he was in his twenties, they provided him with a regular supply of newly-baked clay pipes, which they left for him to collect in the Red Lion at Lowick. The pipes had matured in the burn, so that when the mound was opened they were 'glossy and coal-black, ready to give a cool sweet smoke from the first pipe of tobacco.'

Charcoal burning ceased shortly after Ransome wrote *Swallowdale*, but recently there has been something of a revival of woodland industries. Some years ago the Lake District National Park Authority grant-aided a study of the feasibility of reviving the industry, using portable metal kilns in order to maintain the natural habitat created by coppicing. Burns still take place from time to time in these kilns and the charcoal is sold for use in barbecues. At Stott Park, near the foot of Windermere, the old bobbin mill has become a working museum and some charcoal burning has taken place there. Reconstructed charcoal burners' huts can be seen at Brantwood and in Grizedale Forest. Remains of hearths or pitsteads about six metres in diameter are still to be found in clearings beside old woodland paths in the area.

Cumberland and Westmorland wrestling takes place at some of the Cumbrian shows. Competitors wear traditional costumes consisting of vest, long-johns and lavishly embroidered velvet shorts. The bout begins as the contestants clasp hands behind each other's back and, by intertwining legs, attempt to catch their opponent off balance. It is a sport in which agility is as important as physical strength. When he was staying at Wall Nook farm near Cartmel in his early twenties, Ransome wrestled with the young men practising for the Grasmere Sports.

Fell running is now so popular that it has become a nationally recognised sport, and regular championship events are held. The Guides' Race which Nancy describes, still takes place at the Grasmere Sports that are held on the third Thursday in August. However, it is the smaller shows, less conscious of their ability to attract tourists, that provide the best opportunity to glimpse the world Ransome wrote about in *Swallowdale*. At the Cartmell Show, as well as the animal classes and show jumping, there are hound trails and a display of village industries (including patchwork quilting) in which present-day Mrs Swainsons compete.

Swallowdale is the longest of the stories, largely because Ransome decided to add the surprise attack and Titty's candle-grease witchcraft to his original version. The book was published at the beginning of November 1931 and sold rather better than *Swallows and Amazons*. When it appeared in the United States the following February, he discovered — much to his disgust — that the first chapter had been 'cut to pieces and spoilt by omission of the last three sentences. VERY DAMN INDEED.' But by that time he was hard at work on the second version of *Peter Duck*.

Chapter Seven
PIRATE TREASURE

At the start of 1932 Arthur and Evgenia sailed from Manchester aboard the *Scottish Prince* bound for Alexandria. From there a steamship which called at Cyprus and Mersena in Turkey took them to Alexandretta. Finally they were taken overland to Alleppo where, it was hoped, Ernest Altounyan would be able to cure Ransome's ulcer.

Before they left England Ransome had been busily searching for a dinghy for Ted Scott and his son Dick to sail on Windermere. The boat he found had fitted buoyancy tanks and so was virtually unsinkable. He told Scott that he should call the boat *Amazon*, 'because she is exactly like the little varnished boat that used to be *Swallow's* consort and rival.' Even when writing from Aleppo, he took a keen interest in Scott's new pastime:

Storrs is the best place to live at from the point of view of the little boat. They have a good boathouse, and plenty of sheltered water. There is none at the Wateredge. But the Wateredge is our favourite port of call. It's lovely to sail up there from Bowness, tie up at the little private Wateredge pier, and feed on the lawn with the little boat bobbing at the pier end just below one.

Another thing to do at that end of the lake is to sail and subsequently row up the river. You can get a good long way. Then there is Wray Bay and White Cross Bay (both good perch fishing places)...N.B. Don't take the boat out of the water more than you can help. E.G. Don't take her out of the water except for the actual journey to some other water, unless you have real reasons for so doing. Bad for her.

Don't go and get drowned before I'm there to fish you out!!

There was sailing in Alleppo that year. Ransome had taken a ten-foot dinghy from England so that the Altounyans could sail on the lake near their holiday home. The children called the little boat *Peter Duck* after the new book on which Ransome was working.

Peter Duck had been at the planning stage for more than a year before Ransome began writing the story for a second time. The old seaman, after whom the story is named, was based on his old shipmate, Carl Sehmel. With the wisdom acquired through years at sea, Peter Duck is a welcome and necessary corrective to hasty, romantic Captain Flint. The other newcomer is the red-haired Bill, who claimed to have been born aboard a trawler on the Dogger Bank. His upbringing and outlook on life is utterly different from that of the Swallows and Amazons.

As a boy Peter Duck had been washed ashore on an uninhabited island in the Caribbean Ocean. One morning he heard two men burying a square bag beneath a palm tree, and he followed the men back to their ship. The two who had buried the bag were drowned, and Duck eventually returned to Lowestoft, the only survivor of the wreck. Sixty years later he ships with Captain Flint and his crew of Swallows and Amazons aboard the schooner *Wild Cat*. Peter Duck's story had by then become common knowledge among Lowestoft folk, and a gang of cut-throats had sailed in search of the treasure, only to return empty-handed. Now, across the harbour, the same gang is making ready for another expedition. The voyage of the *Wild Cat* begins as a peaceful cruise down Channel, but soon the ship is embroiled in a full-blown race to Crab Island and a treasure hunt. There is a felicitous ending when the chasing pirate ship is

'John turned the wheel, and the compass card inside the little window just before him moved round.' The ship's wheel and immaculate rigging of the great four-masted sail-training barque **Kruzenshtern** *at Portsmouth in 1998 was a sight that Peter Duck would have savoured.*

caught in a waterspout just as they are attacking the *Wild Cat*.

A brief but memorable episode occurs one dawn when the *Wild Cat* sights a full-rigged ship and Peter Duck is called on deck to enjoy the sight. 'Rot screw steamers,' bursts out the old seaman fiercely, 'Driving vessels like her off the seas where they belong!' Owing to the increasing recognition of the value of sail-training a number of deep-water sailing vessels have survived. One of them, the *Kruzenshtern*, was the last great commercial four-master to be built anywhere in the world when she was launched in Germany as the *Padua* for the Flying P Line of nitrate carriers in 1926. The vessel was acquired by the Russians after the Second World War. Even more encouraging has been the number of new vessels built in

the last twenty years for sail-training. In this country the Jubilee Sailing Trust alone has provided 15,000 able-bodied and physically disabled with the experience of offshore sailing aboard their barque *Lord Nelson*. Ransome and Peter Duck would have thoroughly approved — though perhaps Peter Duck would have been surprised at the number of young and not so young women wanting to enrol. A new and larger ship — 215 feet in length — is being built in Southampton, and something which would delight Peter Duck's heart even more is the construction in Holland of a replica of a mid-nineteenth century clipper ship. With the *Cutty Sark* Tall Ships Races attracting large entries, the future of his beloved tall ships seems secure.

The genesis of the story is to be found among the works of one of Ransome's most admired buccaneers, E. F. Knight. *The Cruise of the Falcon*, published around 1884, is the account of how Knight with three friends and a cabin boy sailed a 28-ton yawl across the Atlantic to South America and cruised up the rivers Parana and Paraguay from Buenos Aires. On their return home, they came to a remote island which is described in the

South Atlantic Directory as 'surrounded by sharp, rugged coral rocks, with an almost continual surge breaking on almost every part, which renders landing often precarious, and watering frequently impractical...the surf is often incredibly great, and has been seen during a S.W. gale to break over a bluff which is 200 feet high.'

The *Falcon's* crew found 'a precipitous mass of barren volcanic rock, with lofty inaccessible summits'. After anchoring off the island, Knight caught a number of rainbow-coloured fish. They landed in the only place where the breakers did not thunder on to the shore and found a land covered with black rocks and loose volcanic ash, as wild and uninviting as its reputation. Wrecks were scattered along the shore and close at hand they found a spring of fresh water. All this appears in *Peter Duck*, but the most remarkable sight were the crabs:

> They were fearful as the firelight fell on their yellow cynical faces, fixed as that of the sphinx, but fixed in a horrid grin...staring at me. Smelling the fish we were cooking, they came down the mountains in thousands upon us...One of us had to keep watch, so as to drive them from the other two, otherwise we should have had no sleep. Imagine a sailor cast alone on this shore, weary, yet unable to sleep a moment on account of these ferocious creatures...

Ransome called the island on which young Peter Duck had been washed ashore Crab Island. By moving it more than 3,000 miles to the edge of the Caribbean Sea, he made it believable for the palm trees to be growing that provided a haven for the boy when he wanted to escape from the crabs at night.

That was not all. In *The Cruise of the Alerte*, published in 1890, Knight told how he had returned to Trinidad and spent three months ashore in search of treasure, reputed to have been buried by pirates in 1821. A treasure map on a piece of tarpaulin had been passed on by a dying 'pirate' to a South Shields opium trader, and by the time Knight set out, there had already been several fruitless expeditions to recover it. Since Knight's quest, there have been several more — all unsuccessful.

In Aleppo Ransome wrote in the mornings and

reached 300 pages quite rapidly. Instalments were read aloud to a most receptive audience. It was, after all, their story in more ways than one, for almost as soon as they had read *Swallows and Amazons*, Dora, Taqui and Titty had suggested that he should write the next book about buried treasure. Titty told him in her letter: 'Make it with a treasure or something hidden somewhere — on an island of course so that there will be something about boats in it — and let the Swallows (that is if you are going to write about them again) find it after a LOT of adventures. And let everyone make a discovery of some sort.' Ransome did his best to comply with the last suggestion: Susan and Peggy discover the treasure itself, Roger finds the pirate knife, Titty finds Duckhaven, Nancy finds the spring and Bill is the first to spot Crab Island on the horizon.

While still in Aleppo, Ransome began to make sketches for the illustrations. When *Swallows and Amazons* had appeared without illustrations, a leading bookseller had the temerity to suggest to Ransome that it ought to be illustrated. He replied gruffly that an artist would be sure to get it all wrong, so he had a good mind to do the illustrations himself. Titty helped him with some of the sketches, but sadly none of her work has survived among his sketchbooks except one loose page with a pen and ink sketch of a doll. There are, however, several fine sketches among the *Peter Duck* trials which it is tempting to see as the work of Dora Altounyan.

The visit started promisingly enough. Evgenia welcomed the escape from winter in the Lake District and Ransome enjoyed playing tennis with the children. Unfortunately Ernest Altounyan was unable to cure Ransome's duodenal troubles, and his health grew steadily worse as tension between the Ransomes and Altounyan increased. Perhaps Ransome was unconsciously jealous of a man who had married into the Collingwood family. At any rate, there had been some criticism of the way the Altounyans were bringing up their children. Eventually there was 'a stand-up row' over some trifling matter, and although afterwards it was patched up, the Ransomes decided to return to England as soon as possible. In mid-April there was an emotional farewell to Dora and the children when they sailed for Cyprus in order to catch a boat for Rotterdam.

On arrival in the Netherlands they received the tragic news of Ted Scott's death. He had attempted to swim ashore from his new dinghy after it had capsized on Windermere. Not only had Ransome lost his closest friend, but he tortured himself with the thought that, but for his influence, Scott would never have taken up sailing.

Ransome stopped off at Lowestoft for a couple of days to make sure of the details for the opening chapter while Evgenia went on ahead to Ludderburn. After spending the night with the Kelsalls, she returned to find that the cottage had been burgled. Although nothing of value had been taken, it was all most unpleasant. Once back home, Ransome continued to work on the sketches. To help him, Colonal Kelsall rigged up makeshift bunks and a capstan, and Ransome took photographs using the Kelsall boys and a couple of local girls as models. He covered 51 pages with sketches and trials for *Peter Duck*. Some of the drawings are more accomplished than those in the finished version for the book, for Ransome was at pains to make the illustrations appear as if Nancy and her friends were responsible for them. To complete the illusion that *Peter Duck* is the work of the Swallows and Amazons the book is dedicated to: 'Mrs Robert Blackett and Mrs E. H. R. Walker...'

Most of June and July that year was spent on revision and, although he had succeeded in convincing himself that it was a failure the book was ready for the publishers at the beginning of August.

In a letter to his mother he said that 'the only thing in it that is much pleasure to me is the development of the characters of Peter Duck and Captain Flint. And of course, my red-haired boy is rather a lark, and a useful change from the others. But I fear people who like the other two books will be horribly disappointed to find this one so different.'

There is something to be said for Ransomes's assessment, yet the book was an instant success and its warm reception ensured the continuation of the series. The metamorphosis of Carl Sehmel into Peter Duck is a triumph.

*Ransome's unused sketch of the cabin in the **Wild Cat** as Peter Duck spun his yarn. Titty and Susan sit on either side of the old seaman while Captain Flint perches on the chart table.*

(Abbot Hall)

Chapter Eight
SIGNALLING TO MARS

P.D. being REPRINTED!!!!! and it's only been out a month — we shall pull through after all. I stand on my cranium.'

The news that *Peter Duck* was a success ushered in a new era in Ransome's life. With the prospect of financial security, he could at last follow Forest Smith's advice and give up journalism for good. 'Books are all right,' he wrote to his mother. 'But I must manage not to have a rush with them.' It would have been more to the point had he written that he must not allow himself to become anxious about producing them. Although he was no longer concerned about the danger of running out of money or having to meet newspaper deadlines, Ransome fretted over the composition of each book and the need to have it ready for the Christmas market. Not infrequently he worked himself up to a state of turmoil. In *Winter Holiday* — one of the most original and appealing of the series — the writing seems so effortless that it is hard to imagine the dreadful struggle that Ransome had during the eight months that he worked on it. Only from his diary and the surviving letters written to his mother and Wren Howard of Jonathan Cape do we know what the book cost him.

After the high romance of *Peter Duck* it is a relief to be back in the familiar lake country once more. One of the book's strengths lies in the evocation of a hard winter in the hills and the re-creation of the frozen lake of 1929 and the Great Frost of 1895 when Ransome was at school in Windermere. The children's adventures are played out against a background which is true to life. The local folk and other visitors may be referred to as Eskimos and seals, but they are seen to have lives of their own and to respond to the frozen lake in

different ways. In the story the doctor puts chains on both back wheels, a local dare-devil skates from end to end of the lake, the blacksmith is kept busy fitting sledge-runners and the farmers are concerned for feeding their sheep.

Nancy plans an expedition to the North Pole and calls for all hands to convert the remains of a bark-peeler's hut into an igloo. When she is laid low with mumps, the others are given an extra month's holiday in quarantine and Peggy is shipped over to Holly Howe in the hope that she will not catch mumps too. The explorers and pirates — now all Arctic explorers — call Wild Cat Island Spitzbergen and Captain Flint's houseboat after the explorer Nansen's ship *Fram*. Finally, after a month of skating and sledging practice, they are going to trek to the head of the lake where Nancy has located the North Pole.

The book's other great virtue is the introduction of the two central characters, Dorothea, aged 12, and her brother Dick who is a year or so younger. They are a couple of city children from an academic background similar to Ransome's and there is the hint that their father is Professor of Archeology at University College, London. Ransome may have realised that the majority of his readers did not have their own dinghies or live in lake country, and that they would identify more readily with his newcomers to the Lake District. Apart from providing a fresh viewpoint, the Ds also gave the series the impetus it needed at the

Two views of Bowness Bay during the short sharp frost of 1929, when for a few days the ice was safe and the Ransomes skated across the lake. (Courtesy Ed Geddard)

Low Yewdale Farm where Ransome stayed as a young man. It is generally agreed to be the model for Dixon's Farm.

time when he was already tiring of his Swallows and Amazons

It is generally agreed that Ransome put a great deal of himself into Dick and Dorothea, although Dot probably also owed something to his sister Joyce, who also became a writer of children's books. Her plaits may have been a tribute to his young friends, Joan and Peggy Hudson, who wore their hair plaited and took the parts of Susan and Titty in the photographs for the *Peter Duck* illustrations.

Ransome was unusually upbeat about his new-comers. 'If people don't like my little astronomer and scientifically minded Dick, I'll eat ten new hats at a sitting.' Of Dorothea he said: 'One of the two new characters you won't be able to help lik-

ing. I find her a most entertaining companion...' Above all, Dorothea provided him with fresh eyes to witness his leading players. She is essentially an imaginative observer, and through her Ransome created some of his most memorable images.

The Ds are staying at Dixon's Farm for the last week of the winter holidays. They signal to and then meet the Swallows who are staying at Holly Howe. Nancy is impressed with their signalling and invites them to join their North Polar Expedition. With the arrival of snow, the D's establish their right to a place in the party by the excellence of their skating. Even after Nancy is laid low with mumps, she remains the prime mover in their later exploits, sending them over the ice to Wild Cat Island and up on the fells where Dick leads the rescue of a starving sheep belonging to Mr Dixon. Next, she arranges for them all to establish their base aboard Captain Flint's empty houseboat. Finally she challenges them to sleep aboard instead of returning to the farm each evening. While the Swallows remember their ancient promise not to sail at night, the Ds have no such pangs of conscience and are caught on board by the returning Captain Flint, who is astonished to find strangers in his cabin. Very soon all is explained and Captain Flint becomes Nancy's ally. It is he who makes all the arrangements for the final dash for the Pole. There is a glorious misunderstanding when Nancy's signal sets the Ds racing for the north a day too soon and they are overtaken by a blizzard.

For Ransome, the year 1933 began well, with visits from the Altounyan children, now at a boarding school in Windermere. However, in the middle of February there occurred the most dreadful row with Ernest Altounyan after Titty had been to stay with the Ransomes for a few days. It seems probable that it was at this time that the Ransomes made some attempt to adopt her. The Altounyans were a very close family and their reaction to such a suggestion can be imagined. A week later Ransome suffered a bad fall on a steep road some distance from the cottage:

> I had had a good morning's work, and after lunch was walking down the steep hill into the valley, when something Roger said so delighted me that, exulting, I whirled my walking stick and came to myself some minutes later lying on my back with my head downhill. Every writer of stories will understand. He works laboriously on to be unexpectedly rewarded by some small windfall or godsend that is enough to send him skipping. Did not the mountains skip like rams? When stout elderly writers do this they are apt to break their ankles. I broke mine on a lonely road with no chance of help, crawled home, fainted again

on the way, and for the next few weeks had to work on *Winter Holiday* in bed.

For a while they believed that his ankle was only badly sprained. At that time the cottage was snowbound and it was a couple of days before the doctor was able to call and it was he who eventually decided that the bone was broken. Even in bed, Ransome managed to write between five and eight pages a day, in spite of confiding in his diary that he was stuck and that there was something 'fundamentally wrong' with the whole book. He even doubted if Dick and Dorothea fitted his 'strange tale'. By March, still plagued with doubts, he buoyed himself up in a letter to his mother:

> The new book is much more difficult than any of the other time; it is going to be a tough job all the way through. And then everybody will curse me for not letting the Swallows and Amazons be the principle characters. They are there all the time, but the main interest is in my new couple...However, if I can get the thing roughed out by the end of April and then forget it on the Broads, I think I ought to be able to pull it into shape in time for the autumn as usual.

In the event, *Winter Holiday* was not finished when the time came to spend three weeks sailing on the Broads with the Kelsalls. It was still unfinished at the beginning of June, when the publish-

The eight Arctic explorers planned to visit the snowy summit of Kanchenjunga on the day that Nancy developed mumps.

ers wanted a descriptive blurb for the cover. So gloomy were his thoughts that not until July did he feel able to oblige Wren Howard:

> Will this do?
>
> I wrote a draft of it some time ago but to tell you the truth did not like to send it because I was so afraid I was not going to get it done in time.
>
> I have now got the whole thing on paper, and am frantically working at the revision, having the usual awful struggle with it.
>
> I do wish to goodness you were a little nearer, to tell me how to work the damned beginning which, as ever, bothers me simply out of my life.

The main problem with the opening appears to have been Dorothea. His cryptic diary entry reads, 'Bad beginning. Dorothea talks too much. Her imaginings should be missed out.' He struggled on, only breaking off when Margaret and Charles Renold stayed at Ludderburn in June. Renold was

Sketch of a wading fisherman from one of Ransome's tiny notebooks. Was this Charles Renold? (Leeds U).

a keen fisherman and Ransome hoped to introduce them to the delights of dinghy sailing. The Renolds camped on one of the Windermere islands (he does not say which one). They were taken out in *Swallow* and taught to sail. A similar dinghy was commissioned at a cost of £21 from Crossfield, the Arnside boatbuilders who had built *Swallow*. After their visit, Ransome returned to work complaining that the book was 'wrong because of the Dick and Dorothea business'.

At the end of June he began an 'almost hopeless revision. 413 pages of appalling, long-winded unrealised bilge. I shall try to squash it down to 330 and see if that will pull it together, but I doubt if owt's any good. 'All through the July heatwave, when farmers were forced to do their haymaking by moonlight for the sake of the horses, Ransome wrestled with the book and managed to squeeze the story into 360 pages. By the beginning of August, he was utterly depressed and felt he was achieving nothing. He confided in his diary that the book was no good and would not be done in time: 'I don't know what I can do to make things better for Genia. It's really that I am old and she is not. Pretty damn miserable at seeing her so wretched.' He was only 49.

Somehow he managed to pull himself together and in the middle of August sent the first fourteen chapters direct to the printers — without the publishers reading or editing them first. It was now the end of the book which occupied his attention. Ten days later the printers were sent the remainder of the text, and he urged Wren Howard to look carefully at the proofs because he was still not happy with the ending. 'I am absolutely blessed if I know what is wrong with it, but I know jolly well that something is wrong...'

Wren Howard was more than encouraging, and Ransome was, 'most awfully pleased' that he liked it. Howard must have suggested that it was a pity to have Molly Blackett (the Amazons' mother) joining the party at the North Pole, for Ransome wrote a spirited defence:

> (1) Captain Flint's attitude is too near the children's to provide sufficient contrast between grown-ups and non grown-ups view of the escapade
> (2) Mothers will think it odd if she goes comfortably to sleep in bed without seeing with her own eyes.

(3) Children who remember the end of *Swallows and Amazons* will think it odd.

(4) Ejecting her will prevent the necessary explanations being made to explain the secrecy.

The publisher also questioned the need for Mrs Blackett to fumigate the bedroom and scorch the package containing the key to the houseboat. Ransome consulted 'the best local doctor' and replied: 'The precautions in the book are those he would himself suggest in cases where there was special reason to take extra care.' All this correspondence took place in mid-September — only six weeks or so before copies of the book were due in the shops for the Christmas market.

Earlier that year Wren Howard had asked Ransome to illustrate *Winter Holiday* himself, probably because the publishers had had enough of Ransome's disapproval of the work of earlier illustrators. Ransome's response was typical. He wrote to his mother: 'Cape insists on my doing my own pictures. Hell!!!' To Wren Howard he was more practical:

> Now look here. In case I am able to illustrate it myself (which I very much doubt) what I want to know is this. Is it possible by present methods to reproduce as ordinary line blocks, on the ordinary printing paper used for printing my books, pictures made by working on TINTED paper...? grey? or brown? by drawing in process white and black? You can see the point is that there is no other way to get such good snow effects. I fancy it can be done...

Jonathan Cape made a note on the letter, 'No. Lots of extra expense and our margin is too thin already.' Instead Wren Howard urged the use of plenty of strong black tone. Ransome replied, 'I will bear in mind what you say about covering as much ground as possible with black ink so that aunts and such feel they're getting good value for money.' Once he had embarked on the drawings, Ransome wanted to hide behind Nancy Blackett and asked for her name to appear on the title page. His publishers did not agree, but allowed the 'Note on the Pictures' thanking Nancy 'for much earnest work on the illustrations of this book.' For his part, Ransome, who always took a keen interest in the book jackets and chose the colour of

each, refused to allow the words 'Illustrated by the Author' to appear in the panel included in the design, so they had to be replaced by 'With many Illustrations.'

Producing the drawings was more time-consuming than Ransome had anticipated. Two sketches a day were all he could manage, and usually the inked versions took two days. He worked carefully with a fine pen and Indian ink on an image that was somewhat larger than the size of the reproductions. 'Ink is hard unyielding stuff,' he complained to his mother. 'I wish I could use watercolour.' The printers were told to leave space for 20 full page pictures. Meanwhile Ransome worked on; '... I shall have to make considerable use of the 11 full pages which now grimace in a row along my bookcases revealing to me every morning new monstrosities of the human form which I had previously not noticed at all...John is my trouble. In two of my best drawings he has turned into a clumsy lad of seventeen. I can't keep him young.' Evgenia was her usual outspoken self, insisting that in future he should only illustrate books about boats and the sea.

For the miniature tailpieces that appear at the ends of chapters he drew some delightful images. He copied sketches by his mother and 'got Barbara to do a kettle and a few other details which I similarly swiped.' The drawings of the hurricane lantern, skaters, medicine bottle, candlestick and sailing sledge are beautifully observed and even the picture of the whimsical polar cake works. Ransome apparently thought otherwise: 'there will be no falling off in money worth for people who like looking at bad drawings.' In the event, Barbara's kettle was not used, but keen-eyed readers might have spotted it on the dust jacket, together with the drawing of a gateway which does not appear elsewhere inside the book.

Finally Ransome told Wren Howard to, 'throw out the lot' if he wanted. Anticipating that some would be rejected, he had provided more illustrations than the printers were expecting, and when none were returned, he wrote back, 'Hi! I expected you to hurl forth the worst of these...What about that niggly one of them being capsized in the snowstorm? My wife says that picture is a disgrace and I ought never to have let you see it. I only let it go because I had nowt better and because a small girl liked it.'

The *Winter Holiday* saga had a happier ending than Ransome could have foreseen, for 1,500 copies were sold on publication day — as many as *Swallowdale* had sold in its first year. By Christmas the sales had reached almost 5000 copies. Speaking at the Authors Club, the Duke of Kent made special mention of the illustrations, and Cape immediately used the quote on the reprint dust jacket. 'What did Prince George say?' wrote Ransome. 'But whatever he said the use of it made by you was wholly admirable in browbeating my missis into taking a kinder view of my illustrator.'

Of all the incidentals in the book that were taken from life, the most interesting was the signalling arrangement between Dixon's Barn and Holly Howe by means of square and triangular shapes hoisted up the walls. This was the very system which had been in use for some time between Ludderburn and Barkbooth where the Kelsalls lived. The Colonel devised the code mainly as a means of communicating fishing messages, since Ludderburn was not on the telephone. By the time of *Winter Holiday* it had been expanded to provide a possible 74 variations.

In the story Mrs Dixon recalls the Great Frost of 1895 when frozen Windermere became such an attraction that train-loads of visitors arrived on day excursions, and brass bands and gramophones played for the skaters and dancers. One observer, writing in the *Westmorland Gazette*, estimated that there were around 2,000 skaters on the ice around Bowness Bay. But the ice also brought hardship to the area, for many labourers and wall-builders were unable to work; in Kendal large quantities of soup were distributed to the most needy residents. Arthur, who was at school in Windermere during the Great Frost, remarks in his *Autobiography* that the days when the boys were allowed to skate on the ice were the happiest he had spent during his time there. Perhaps that was why he confessed to having 'a sort of tenderness' for a book that looked back to those experiences, in spite of all that it had cost him to produce.

The igloo seems to have been built upon a bark-peeler's hut. These were circular or oval in shape with low stone walls and a hearth at the rear. There are the remains of several bark peelers' as well as charcoal burners' huts among the steep woods which run along the eastern shore of Coniston Water. Perhaps Ransome had in mind the fine example which stands within sight of the road, a little to the north of Peel Island. The peeler and his family lived in the hut during high summer when oak bark could be peeled easily. The bark was used for tanning leather and there were tanneries in most of the lakeland towns and villages in Ransome's time.

Dixon's Farm, which had been no more than a

Three of Winter Holiday's *delightful tailpieces.*

A possible igloo can be found among the woods a little north of Peel Island and may be spotted without leaving the road. (Ted Alexander)

source of supplies and gossip in earlier books, takes the form of Low Yewdale Farm, north of Coniston where Ransome had lodged in 1908. High Greenland, where Dick rescued the sheep, resembles the fells above Nibthwaite to the east of Coniston Water. The sheep was particularly unlucky to have become cragfast so far from home for crags of that sort are not to be found among the Silurian rocks of the Coniston-Windermere area. Dick's rescue was repeated in 1994 when a pack of 24 hounds became trapped on St Sunday Crag near Patterdale. The dogs had to spend a night on the ledge before each dog was lowered to the ground by means of a rope sling.

The North Pole itself remains the most elusive of all the places in the books, perhaps because Ransome so successfully camouflaged the source of his inspiration, or because the building has vanished without trace. The Turret Room at Brantwood is a possibility. From there Ruskin could look out at a magnificent view in all weathers whilst remaining indoors. Alternatively, the octagonal garden house, now known as Storrs Temple, has its supporters. It was erected at the end of a stone causeway built out into

Windermere in 1804 to commemorate Admirals Duncan, Howe, Vincent and Nelson. At present the arched openings are unglazed, but perhaps the glass was removed at some time.

Set in the grass at Borrans Park at the head of Windermere there is a tablet identifying the site of the North Pole. Enthusiasts have marked the position of a building which they claim was shaped like the North Pole, standing near the shore. Appropriately, it was identified by means of a divining rod, but so far no independent supporting evidence of such a building has come to light. The site stands close to a former footpath that ran alongside a stone wall leading to a jetty that has since disappeared. The wall has gone as well, but its course is clearly visible in the right light. However, the first rough sketches of Nancy reaching the Pole shows the building high above her, more or less where a Victorian conservatory used to stand on the facade of Wanlass Howe, overlooking the park and with a clear view down the lake.

The strongest reason for casting doubt on the 'perfect solution' of an identical building in the actual location within a public park is that it is completely out of character, for Ransome took such great pains to keep his locations a secret. Probably we shall never know for certain. Anyway, as Peggy Blackett said of the preparations for the North Pole, 'It only spoils things to be too beastly clever.'

The book is dedicated to 'The Clan McEoch' of Massachusetts, U.S.A. Countless children have played at Swallows and Amazons, including, we are told, Her Majesty the Queen and Princess Margaret, but the McEochs wrote to tell Ransome

that they were ashamed of being Swallows and Amazons and had invented a ploy of their own.

(Opposite, top)
A wintry scene similar to the one which greeted the Ds on their first morning.

(Lower)
*The head of the Windermere where the Ransome's often called to take tea on the lawn of the Wateredge Hotel after having sailed up the lake in **Swallow**. At the extreme left of the picture is the area where the North Pole was situated.*

SWALLOWS·AND·AMAZONS·FOR·EVER!

Chapter Nine
THE HULLABALOOS

Arthur Ransome's introduction to the Norfolk Broads took place in October 1914 when he spent a week pike fishing during one of his trips home from Russia. His next visit was with Ernest Altounyan in the autumn of 1923. He made good use of these experiences when he began the early version of the sequel to *Swallows and Amazons*.

Shortly after Christmas, Captain Flint and the Swallows and Amazons are aboard a wherry, the *Polly Ann*. The weather is so cold that even with the expert assistance of the *Polly Ann's* attendant, Peter Duck, their sailing is severely curtailed. To amuse themselves, they begin the story of the treasure-hunting voyage to Crab Island. Two draft chapters were published in Christina Hardyment's *Arthur Ransome and Captain Flint's Trunk* in 1984. The brief sketch of winter on the Broads is as evocative as the lakeland landscape in *Winter Holiday*:

Next morning there was another cold raw fog lying low over the fens. From only a dozen yards away on the dyke nothing of the *Polly Ann* could be seen but the top of her mast and the upper parts of her shrouds and her forestay, from which the lantern was hanging, glittering feebly in the clear air above the mist...The ropes were stiff and white with hoar frost, and Captain Flint and Peter Duck between them had a hard time in hoisting the wherry's great sail, even with the other two captains, Nancy and John, making the most of their weight...The fog lifted with the easterly wind, and the sun shone out. They cast off from the bank and began to move up river, between the sparkling frosted sedges at the river sides. As the *Polly Ann* moved up the river, the wake she left astern of her sent its ripples to the sedges, and all the

way up the river there was a long tinkling as the ripples broke the cat ice among the reeds.

In the spring of 1931 the Ransomes hired a two-berth cabin yacht, the *Welcome* from Herbert Woods of Potter Heigham, and Ted Scott and his son Dick hired *Winsome*, her sister ship. In an unpublished part of his Autobiography Ransome describes the cruise:

Our first boat on the Broads was one of the last two built by old Walter Woods of Potter Heigham. She was hardly larger than the old *Kittywacky*, but much more comfortable. She was Una-rigged with a gaff sail and her mast stepped close to her bows. She drew so little water that she could make her way up any ditch, and in her we explored thoroughly the whole of the Broads north of Yarmouth. Our favourite time for the Broads was immediately after the Easter holiday, when, in those days, the motor cruisers were for the most part lying unused and waiting for the summer. It was also the best time for the birds. We could see the bearded tits, the big hawks over Hickling and Horsey, hear the booming of the bittern and sometimes see one flying low over the reeds, and very soon found that the birds have made up their minds that sailing boats are harmless. A rowing boat or a motor boat will frighten them from afar, but slipping silently by in a sailing boat or dinghy we were able to photograph great crested grebes on their nests and to watch, from only a few yards away, the parent birds swimming with the young ones on their backs, shrugging off first one and then another to take a swimming lesson.

There was no Broads sailing the following year, but if it had not been for Ted Scott's untimely

Evgenia

death they would all have gone cruising as soon as the Ransomes returned from Syria. In May 1933, they hired a *Fairway* yacht from Jack Powles of Wroxham for three weeks. These were new craft, three feet longer than *Welcome*, and with much greater headroom. The Kelsalls hired *Welcome* at the same time and they met and frequently sailed in company. Ransome was enthusiastic about the *Fairways*:

These boats are 24 feet long, sloop-rigged, with berths for three in two cabins, and the cooking is done under an awning set up at evening over the well using the boom as a roof-tree. We found ourselves cramped for two days, but after that lived in great comfort and once even had Molly Hamilton with us as a passenger. The boats are decently fast, and we had a regular programme. Starting from Wroxham we visited every corner of the Northern Broads and rivers in the first week...Then going down with the tide we came to Yarmouth at low water, worked through the bridges, sailed up Breydon Water, and during the next week went to Oulton Broad, to

Beccles, back to Reedham, and up the Yare to Norwich. Then back again to Yarmouth and with a rising tide up the Bure to Acle, to spend a third week of idle pottering in the easy waters of the north.

The southern waters are of a different character. Thames barges go up the Waveney to Beccles, and coasting steamers follow the Yare up to the iron works at Norwich. You cannot there tie up to the bank wherever you happen to be, but must make up your mind to reach one of the regular places where you can lie in safety, where there are no sunken piles and where you can take precautions against the wash of a passing steamer. This is no real disadvantage. Some of our happiest memories are of slipping along in the dusk, using the last of the tide to bring us to a distant staithe when, in northern waters, we should long ago have been tied up and cooking supper. Being there as often as we did, we came to know the Broads extremely well and to feel very much at home there. In the sixteenth century one of my ancestors was a miller at North Walsham and he may have helped to make me feel no stranger.

He had by then made up his mind that the next book would be set on the Broads and that he had done with his Swallows and Amazons. It was not

(Opposite)
Oulton Broad.

(This page, top)
Beccles Staithe. The
Teasel *and the barge*
Welcome *were moored
to the further bank.*

(Right)
*The New Cut which was
dug in 1833 joins the
Rivers Yare and Waveney.
The old lifting bridge at
Haddiscoe has been
replaced by a fixed bridge
and tolls are no longer
collected by means of a
butterfly net.*

"FAIRWAY" Class (Wroxham)
"Fairway" 3 to 10.
TO SLEEP 3

Length. 23ft. Beam. 7ft. 8ins. Draught. 2ft. 6ins. Headroom. 5ft. 11ins. Rig. Sloop-rig but will sail equally well with or without jib. Cooking. Primus with special cooking locker in well. Lighting. Electric. Berths. Three Somnus spring-berths—third berth is in separate forward cabin. Other features. Carvel-built of mahogany, bright varnish finished.

Teak fittings throughout. Full-length centre-section cabin top lifts both ends. The wash-basin and patent self-emptying W.C. are in a separate compartment with sliding door. Drawers under berths and excellent cupboard and wardrobe space. Well 5ft. 7ins. long and movable saloon table can be used in cabin or well. Awning covers well and boat to the mast. The sailing qualities are excellent and the craft are easily handled. Dinghy provided

A £12 0s. B £14 0s.
including full insurance.
For A and B periods, see page 6.
Deposit required on booking, £3 0s. a week.

PAGE 24

"DELIGHT" Class
"Delight" 1, 3, 5, 7, 9 & 11 (Potter Heigham)
TO SLEEP 3

Length. 24ft. Beam. 8ft. 6ins. Draught. 2ft. Headroom. 6ft. Power. 4-cylinder Morris "Vedette" marine engine with self-starter. Cooking. Calor gas stove and oven. Forward galley with sink, freshwater tank, lockers, and shelves. Lighting. Electric. Berths. Three spring-berths—one forward; two in saloon. Other features. Completely and comfortably equipped with excellent internal arrangements, these craft

afford all the amenities of larger cruisers. Separate toilet compartment with W.C. and wash basin. The saloon is fitted with sideboards, drawer and locker facilities and plate-glass adjustable and removable windows. Exceptionally manœuvrable, the centrally situated controls afford the helmsman a feeling of absolute confidence with all-round vision and instantaneous command over speed and direction. The special folding canopy with side curtains assures comfort in all weathers. Sailing dinghy provided.

A £18 5s. B £21 5s.
including full insurance.
For A and B periods, see page 6.
Deposit required on booking, £4 10s. a week.

PAGE 04

(Left)
The Ransomes' favourite Broads yachts from Blakes catalogue of 1947.
(Courtesy Blakes Holidays Ltd).

(Right)
The Delight class were popular with hirers and remained in the hire fleet for more than thirty years. In many respects they were a miniature version of the dreaded Margoletta.
(Courtesy Blakes Holidays Ltd).

until the middle of September that he could begin to think of anything other than *Winter Holiday* and at the end of the month he went on a fishing holiday with Charles and Margaret Renold:

He was then managing director of a firm which makes bicycle and other chains for all the world. She was that rare being in whom authors find it hard to

believe. She was a reader who never wanted to write a book, and one who, if she liked a book, used instantly to go to a bookshop and send copies to all her friends. We were very fond of both of them and I had turned Charles into a fisherman, and not a mere flyfisher, but one who shared my pleasure in the sort of fishing I had had in Russia, float fishing for course fish. Now there is no better course fishing than on the Broads in autumn and we had planned to go there hiring a motor cruiser (our object being fishing, not sailing) with a sailing dinghy however, in case of backsliding on my part. I reached Manchester feeling ill, but thought it was my usual trouble and that the salt air of the east coast would put me right.

They hired the motor cruiser *Delight* from Herbert Woods' boatyard and motored as far as Kendal Dyke, after stopping to arrange to collect the milk from a farm just above Potter Heigham. A regular supply of milk was essential to keep Ransome's stomach problems at bay. The following day he sailed off in the dinghy to fetch the milk, leaving Renold fishing from the moored cruiser. On the return journey, Ransome gave an extra hard pull on the dinghy's halyard and, 'it was as if some villain had stabbed me in the vitals. I collapsed in the bottom of the boat and could not get up.'

Somehow Ransome managed to sail back to Kendal Dyke and the *Delight*. Masterfully, Renold took charge and insisted on his friend seeing a doctor at the earliest opportunity. He started the engine and set off for Potter Heigham. The proprietors of the inn, fearing something contagious, flatly refused to accept Ransome as a guest. Infuriated, Renold, who had never had charge of such a boat before, motored down the River Thurne and up the Bure to Wroxham, arriving after dark. A doctor was called while Ransome was put to bed at the King's Head, surrounded by hot water bottles. That night he was operated on for acute appendicitis, and underwent another operation a week later after complications had set in. His tribulations brought a sympathetic note from Ivy, saying how 'awfully sorry' she was to hear of his illness and all the pain he was suffering. Evgenia shut up Ludderburn and Ransome completed his recovery by spending two months at St Mawes in Cornwall, where he began thinking about his next book. He wrote to his mother, enthusing about 'rivers and hiding places in the dykes and the little stretches of open water. Really a lovely setting, with herons and bitterns, and fish, very wild except in the holiday months.'

Soon after arriving at St Mawes, he appealed to Margaret Renold for help:

> I've got masses of nice detail to use, but until I get a thread of plot I daren't begin playing with the details. It would only mean hell to pay later...as happened with WH....If you want me to be free for playing about next summer you must at once come to the rescue with a plot for my Broads book.
> Characters: Admirable old lady in houseboat
> Two small girls, (twins, children of local inhabitant...crew of racing dinghy (his) but detached from him in their relation with
> Boy (principal boy and main thread of tale)
> Half a dozen other boys (supers) (useful as signallers...)

Two other girls contrasting with the twins by being generally proper careful gentle creatures but quite all right inside

The book was to be an account of the conversion of two prim and proper town children by their lively Broads-sailing grandmother and her web-footed young friends, and called 'Webfooted Grandmother'. He planned it as a cruise book and had 'masses of thing to happen': there would be shopping at Roy's store, a night spent with an eelman (which he eventually used in *The Big Six*), and a boy casting adrift a boat with someone on board. In the ensuing chase, the crew of a nearby boat would become accomplices to his escape.

Shortly afterwards, Ransome wrote to the Renolds again telling them how his planning had developed. The characters were taking shape. There was to be a Principal Boy, aged about 12 or 13 and living in Horning, and a pair of sailing twins who have to leave their father, with whom they sail, in order to take part. The 'most spirited old lady' was to play a central role. She was to be a widow who paints in water colours and who invites the well-brought-ups to stay for their summer holidays in order that they might be stimulated into becoming more lively. The water-colourist sounds like a clear reference to his mother.

Some sort of collective triumph would be needed in order to bring off a happy and unexpected ending. He mused over the difficulties of involving such a large cast:

> Concentrating the interest on ONE character, in the manner honoured by time and by almost all tellers of stories for boys, is easy but doesn't meet my views. I must have a combination of collective interest and a fair share of the game for all the individuals, girls and boys. Sordid grasp at as wide an audience as possible.
>
> Essential, or all but essential to have one or more characters definitely younger than the rest. Otherwise the whole lot are themselves too conscious of infancy in comparison with the other group of characters who are grown up, Shove in a brat, and the rest gain independence at once.
>
> Golly, what a lot of secrets I am giving away.

At the centre of Ransome's art is his genius as a story-teller, and this letter to Margaret Renold

(Opposite, top)
One of the beautiful **Hustler**
*yachts approaching Horning Hall
Farm which was one of Ransome's
favourite places to moor for the
night.*

(Lower)
*The traditional Broads cruiser that
became famous as the
Hullabaloos' noisy* **Margoletta** *in
the 1984 BBC film of* **Coot Club.**
(Ted Alexander)

(This page, top)
*The wide expanse of Breydon
Water where passing craft are
keeping to the marked channel
even though it is near high water.*

(Right)
From the cockpit of a **Hunter**
*yacht sailing across the open
waters of Barton Broad,*

allows us to overhear some of the thought that went into the crafting of *Coot Club*.

The beginning had been planned before he seriously considered putting Dick and Dorothea in the tale: 'The Propers in the train from Norwich to Wroxham... in corner of carriage Tom with pot of paint?' In spite of his determination to have done with his Swallows and Amazons, he began to realise the possibilities of allowing the new book to grow out of *Winter Holiday*.

Winter Holiday had closed with Dick's brave attempt to sail his sledge. What if in the next book the Ds were to learn to sail on the Broads? On 6th March he decided to replace the Propers with the Ds and on the same day complained to the Renolds 'My book is too elaborate, and too thrutched up. It won't go at all.' Nevertheless he was still completing a steady six pages or so each day.

In May, the Ransomes hired the *Fairway* again and for three weeks followed the cruise of the fictional *Teasel*, checking details and taking photographs from which to make the illustrations. He visited a Dr Long in Norwich and learned from him that the nest of a water rail was too difficult to see. 'Better coot or waterhen. Waterhen nests in bushes or trees or rushes. Coot in the water. Plumped for coot'. So the story became Coot Club, which does sound rather better than 'Water-rail Club'!

By the middle of July the first draft was ready for 'The Critic on the Hearth', Her verdict was: 'Too solid. Not enough dialogue. Not properly realised.' Ransome launched himself into some frantic revision. In September, when he had completed his final version, he still feared the book was 'hopeless', an assessment with which Evgenia agreed, for she told him it would be better not to proceed with the publication. Wren Howard pointed out that it was a dangerous decision. The book had been widely announced, orders were pouring in and a delay until the spring would create a lot of disappointed readers accustomed to their Ransome book at Christmas. He bravely told Ransome that he was over particular and Mrs Ransome was hypercritical. The publisher prevailed, and in November the book appeared in the shops. It was an instant success and became the first Ransome book to sell more than 5000 copies before Christmas.

None of the problems seem to have arisen from writing a story set in an accurately observed setting, and the book benefits greatly from its fidelity and from being firmly rooted in a living landscape. The members of the Coot Club are seen to exist alongside the other Broadland dwellers and boat-owners, unlike the exclusive society of Swallows and Amazons.

The illustrations presented few of the difficulties encountered in *Winter Holiday*. Ransome had numerous photographs to copy, and this gave him the realism for which he strived. He covered almost 80 pages of his sketchbooks with trial sketches. Now that he was able to concentrate on drawing boats once more, he began to tackle his work with greater confidence. Of the finished illustrations, the evening scenes, 'First night in the *Titmouse*' and 'Tied up for the Night' are among the most accomplished.

Ransome kept to his original opening and the Ds meet Tom on the train on their way to stay with Mrs Barrable, an elderly friend of their mother's who is living aboard a yacht, the *Teasel*. They are looking forward to learning to sail and are devastated to find that she has no such plans. When they all become the willing accomplices who assist Tom's flight from the vengeful crew of frightful Hullabaloos, Mrs Barrable sees to it that Tom, who has broken the golden rule of the Broads — don't become involved with foreigners — breaks it once more and takes over as skipper of the *Teasel*. Tom is also aided by his neighbours, twins Port and Starboard, and three young pirates who are all members of a bird protection group called The Coot Club.

It is not devilment which makes Tom cast off the Hullabaloos but rather as a last resort when they refuse to move their mooring away from the unhatched chicks of a special nesting bird. The *Teasel* becomes a training ship, and after sailing the northern Broads, she sets off for southern waters on a pilgrimage to Beccles so that Mrs Barrable may return to her childhood haunts. Ransome had already decided that the Hullabaloos should 'wander in and out from chapter to chapter, so that there is always a danger of Tom being recognised by them. This would give a sort of feeling of outlawry to Tom and to a lesser degree to the three pirates.' The twins' loyalty to their widowed father prevents them from sailing south with the *Teasel*, but when the opportunity arises, they chase after Tom aboard a trading wherry and a Thames barge. During their cruise in 1933, the Ransomes moored alongside the barge *Pudge* at Beccles and were invited aboard. Their time aboard was put to good use in the story where *Pudge* was turned into the *Welcome* of Rochester. The barge was built in 1922 for the London and Rochester Trading Company. The vessel is still earning her keep, being operated by the Thames Barge Sailing Club for charter work and weekend sailing. Finally, the story ends with the Hullabaloos, still intent on vengeance, having to be rescued from drowning on Breydon Water by the heroic pirates who have rowed down river in their *Death and Glory* all the way from Horning.

Soon after their arrival in Norfolk the Ds encounter a group of white-sailed racing boats from Horning Sailing Club. These were yachts of the Yare and Bure One-Design, more commonly known as White Boats, which were designed in 1908 by Ernest Woods, a prolific builder of Broadland craft who had his own boatyard in Horning at the time Ransome was sailing on the Broads. The many White Boat survivors are maintained in immaculate condition by their loving owners and still race regularly at Horning and Wroxham. Traditionally, the boats are said to be named after butterflies, but there were at least three exceptions to this rule — as well as Mr Farland's *Flash* in Coot Club.

At the centre of Coot Club is the *Teasel* herself. She does not seem to have been based upon any particular vessel, but to be entirely typical of the kind of cabin yacht offered for hire in the 1930s — a sort of four-berth version of Ransome's favourite *Fairway*. In the last few years there has been a revival of interest in sailing cruisers and several boatyards have some vintage yachts or vessels with a traditionally-styled glassfibre hull and wooden superstructure among their hire fleet.

Pride of place must go to the magnificent two, three and four-berth yachts of the well-known Hunter Fleet which were almost all built before the Second World War. They were operated by Percy Hunter and his family from their Ludham yard until his death in 1966. The Norfolk County Council then bought out the family and operated the fleet to develop youth sail training — an enterprise which would have been very close to Ransome's heart. When the County Council decided to sell off the fleet and yard in 1995 there was a public outcry. The name Ransome frequently appeared in publicity generated by the *Eastern Daily Press*, and with support from many people who had been introduced to Broads sailing by Ransome, the Norfolk Heritage Fleet Trust was formed. Around a third of the necessary £300,000 was donated by the public and the future of the fleet was secured by a grant of £200,000 from the Heritage Lottery Fund. The thirteen beautiful mahogany cabin yachts closely resemble the Teasel. They have no engines and still use the original cabin oil lamps. One concession to progress has been the installation of a bottled gas stove to replace the old primus stove. The yachts are available for hire to the general public and this enables the youth groups using the craft to be heavily subsidised.

What distinguishes *Coot Club* is its central theme which exposes the conflict between the increasing number of pleasure-seekers and the need to care for an environmentally sensitive area. Archive films show that the Hullabaloos charging down the river with their gramophone blaring, years before anyone had heard of noise pollution, were not merely the product of Ransome's imagination. The *Fairway* had been bumped by a motor cruiser which had refused to give him room when he was sailing on Horning Reach, and as a result the boat had needed some new varnish. Was it this incident which gave him the idea of the Hullabaloos? In any case, the *Margoletta*, full of noisy, carefree pleasure-seekers, was as true to its time as the diminishing fleet of wherrys and the last of the Thames barges sailing up to Beccles.

The Yarmouth tug boat *Come Along* and her skipper Old Bob were real enough, as the log of Ransome's 1933 cruise reveals: 'Old Barbar with his motor tug *Surprise* was waiting, warned by Johnson, well above Breydon swing bridge.'

Only rarely did Ransome depart from an otherwise faithful portrait of the Broads. Dr Dudgeon's house cannot be found in Horning Reach, although the doctor himself was probably based on Dr Bennett of Wroxham, who had rushed to

(Above)
A young fisherman at Horsey Mere tries his luck close to where the Teasel *moored for the night.*

(Left)
The tall sails of the pleasure wherries are still a familiar sight along the northern rivers.

Ransome's aid when he had appendicitis. Mr Tedder, whose gardening is disturbed by the Hullabaloos ranting on Horning Staithe, is Ransome's own creation; the Horning policeman's cottage was actually in Ludham in those days.

The Norfolk Broads are the remains of the pits made by digging for peat that was used locally for fuel in mediaeval times. As the sea level rose, so the pits filled with water and were linked by artificial channels to the natural river system. Today the name is used to include 130 miles of shallow lakes and rivers. When Ransome first visited the Broads, the region was entering a period of transition. Even as early as 1916, potential hullabaloos hiring from H. Blake and Co's Yachting List were recommended to bring a Pathephone phonograph to add to the pleasures of boating. The day of the old-style marshmen, watermen and eel-fishers was almost over and the increasing popularity of boating holidays was attracting the wrong kind of visitor. The wreckers of Yarmouth were known to target privately owned craft, but very little evidence of their activities appears to have survived. There is certainly scope for further research into their nefarious activities.

In Ransome's time the water was sparkling clear, but due to increased phosphate from sewage and nitrates draining from the adjacent farmland, the rivers today are cloudy and some of the Broads have almost silted up. The large glassfibre cruisers and speedy day-boats with their high bow-waves have been responsible for increased erosion and the loss of reed-fringed banks. The situation became so bad by the end of the 1970s that the whole area was under threat and the future of the Broads was in doubt.

Fortunately the area has been well served by environmentalists, and most notably by the naturalist, writer and broadcaster Ted Ellis, whose influence has been profound. Ransome recognised the problem of reconciling the increasing numbers of holidaymakers with the need to care for wildlife, and in *Coot Club* he posted a warning notice for those who could read it. He was not alone, for The Norfolk Naturalists' Trust is the oldest local organisation of its kind in the country. The Trust owns a number of important sites, including parts of Barton Broad, Ranworth Broad and Cockshoot

Broad near Horning. In 1981 the Broads Authority isolated the waters of Cockshoot Broad from the River Bure by means of a dam at the entrance to the dyke and pumped the mud out. When they started, the water was only 15cm deep in places and was unable to support any wild-life to speak of. The regeneration is now complete, and visitors in summer can park or moor at the Ferry Inn and cross by the recently restored passenger ferry to the southern bank of the River Bure where a boardwalk leads past the site of No. 7 coot's nest to the dyke, with its white waterlilies crowning the surface of a magnificent wildlife habitat. A more ambitious scheme of reclamation is being carried out at Barton Broad, which has been the scene of similar pumping operations during the last few years.

Fortunately, following the Broads Plan of 1987 and the belated award of National Park status in 1988, the situation has improved, but it is a fragile environment and the Broads Authority faces the difficult task of balancing the needs of recreation, ecology and agrarian interests. Nowadays, a few folk still carry on the old Broadland traditions in a modern world. Apart from the museums and heritage trails, the past lives on in odd corners of the Broads, and baskets are still made of supple osier and willow, Norfolk reed-thatch is still in demand, a few wooden boats are under construction, and eel-catchers still carry out their nightly solitary vigil.

Ransome's description of the eelman's old houseboat and of the wherry *Sir Garnet* 'shooting' a bridge are historical documents in themselves. His ear for 'Broad Norfolk' was as keen as for the lake country dialect. Jim Woodall remarks: 'Fare to me that George he want 'em to cotch young Tom, but he nat'rally don't want to be in it hisself. So he send 'em where he think they can't fail for to meet him...'

The wherry evolved over a period of several hundred years as the most efficient form of sailing carrier to operate on the narrow and shallow waters. Their cargoes were those goods essential to the well-being of the local economy — coal, reeds, farm produce, bricks, timber and occasionally passengers. They were clinker-built with a single mast set well forward in a tabernacle and counterbalanced by one and a half tons of lead fastened to its base. Several hundred wherries were sailing in the middle of the nineteenth century before the railways and motor transport gradually took away their cargoes. By the end of the First World War only a handful were still struggling to trade under sail.

Nowadays, the wherry *Albion*, owned by the Norfolk Wherry Trust, is a familiar sight as she takes parties sailing on the Norfolk rivers. *Albion* is the only 'Black-sailed Trader' still afloat, although there is a wherry graveyard at Surlingham Broad and a number of wherry hulls have been sunk at other places. One of these, the *Maud* was raised, and after years of devoted restoration she will soon be sailing again. No wherry ever carried the name *Sir Garnet*, although a wherry called *Garnet* was built in Beccles around the middle of the nineteenth century. Ransome saw a wherry with the name *Lord Roberts* at Horning in 1934, and this may have inspired him to choose to name his creation after Sir Garnet Wolseley, a distinguished soldier who had been a childhood hero.

When holiday-makers first began to hire boats, some of the wherries had their holds swept out and beds, chairs and chests-of-drawers put in for the summer season. The cooking was done by the skipper and his mate who also acted as steward. As holidays of this kind became more popular, some craft were permanently converted by covering the hold and adding bulkheads to divide up the space below. These conversions were so successful that more than 30 purpose-built pleasure wherries joined the fleet, and by 1900 there were more than 100 available for hire. The pleasure wherries *Solace* and *Hathor* and wherry yachts *Olive*, *White Moth* and *Norada* are still in full sailing order and available for charter.

Coot Club is dedicated to 'The Skipper of the Titmouse.' Since Ransome was hardly likely to have chosen to dedicate the book to a fictitious person, the question remains, who was this anonymous sailor? Was Dr Bennett a sailing man? Or Blaxland, the surgeon who conducted the operation? Perhaps Dick Scott had sailed a dinghy named *Titmouse* during the holiday he had spent with his father and the Ransomes on the Broads in 1931?

Chapter Ten
ALL THAT GLITTERS

In January 1935 Ransome drove to Teignmouth in Devon to see his first wife, Ivy, so that he might learn more about their daughter's recent marriage. Ivy confided her anxiety over dinner and their mutual concern for Tabitha's happiness seems to have brought peace at last between Arthur and Ivy. Tabitha had married a 'rough diamond', and Ransome was very disturbed by the marriage: 'I went to bed so sick I could not sleep.'

Ivy wrote a little later, after further acquaintance with Tabitha's husband:

> My Dear Arthur
> ...He is 'not on the make'...He is straight, clean, honest and has all the decent instincts...he is content to be ordered about by Tabbie — morning, all day and all night she orders him and he obeys. He can 'double-shuffle' with his feet like a variety showman, he can lift a sack of potatoes above his head, he never tells a dirty story...he never takes advice amiss, he is never presumptuous, nor cringing — just natural...
> Your placid ex-wife Constance

As if to emphasise that the breach had been healed, Ivy generously agreed to limit her financial claims to £100 p.a. and this money she passed to Tabitha.

From the few notes that have survived, it appears that Ransome did not begin work on *Pigeon Post* until March. The inspiration for the new story had come from the mining activities of his friend Oscar Gnosspelius, who had married the sculptor Barbara Collingwood. The couple had settled at High Hollin Bank at the head of Coniston Water. A man of varied talents and interests, Gnosspelius had been an aircraft inventor and had worked abroad in Peru and Africa as a survey-or and civil engineer. Over tea at Low Ludderburn in February, he had furnished Ransome with some accurate mining details, although there is nothing to suggest that he also provided the plot. Barbara, who had succeeded her father as President of the Lake Artists' Society, was on hand to give advice on some of the illustrations, but it is extremely doubtful if her work appears in the book

A few weeks later Gnosspelius took Ransome up behind Tilberthwaite Ghyll, where he showed him several of the old copper mine workings. Under the slopes of the mountain is a wild plateau, half circled by the fells, which he thought would be a suitable setting for the goldfields in the story. In June they went further up the mountain above Swallow Scar. 'I got pretty awfully tired, and duodenum got a bit stirred up,' Ransome's diary tells us. 'I thought I was going to be sick, but wasn't. Very jolly up there among the screes.'

Pigeon Post opens at the beginning of the summer holiday. Captain Flint is abroad, looking for gold, and Nancy and Peggy miss their father-figure. They think that if they can find him some gold in the lake country, he will want to remain at home in future. Once the Swallows, Amazons and Ds are assembled at Beckfoot, they consult a local miner, Slater Bob, who tells them of a legend about gold in the nearby hills. The explorers and pirates, now turned mining prospectors, find that the goldfields are some distance away. After a lot of persuasion, Mrs Blackett allows them to leave Beckfoot on the understanding that they send home a daily message by pigeon post. When a mysterious stranger appears they believe that he is also after the gold, and this changes what might have been something of a game into more serious business. It has been an unusually dry summer, and because of the

(This page, top)
Under the shoulder of Wetherlam lies the plateau that Ransome called High Topps.

(Left)
'Very jolly up there among the screes,' Ransome confided in his diary after visiting Swallow Scar on Wetherlam.

(Opposite, top)
Coppermines Valley. In the 19th century the area provided a living for several hundred workers.

(Lower)
The River Amazon changes its character in the upper reaches beside the narrow winding road along which the prospectors trekked on their way to Tyson's Farm. It closely resembles Tilberthwaite Beck flowing along the Tilberthwaite valley.

The sight of the distant hills beyond the village of Windermere greeted Titty and Roger as they arrived at the start of **Pigeon Post.**

drought, the only possible camp-site is in the orchard of Tysons farm, down in the valley below the goldfields. If they are to be the first to find the gold, it is essential to be closer at hand in a hill-top camp within easy access of drinking water.

Dick raises their hopes when he sees rushes growing in an ideal camp-site and sets them all dowsing for water. When Titty discovers she has the gift it is such a devastating experience that the others agree not to ask her to dowse again. However, Titty believes that the success of the enterprise depends on her finding an underground spring and so secretly she takes the forked hazel

twig in her hands once more and discovers the source of water they need.

Eventually Roger finds the gold and there is plenty of real-life adventure — fending off the 'enemy', fighting a fell fire and explorers trapped underground. When Captain Flint returns, the prospectors learn that their hated rival is actually his partner, and the 'gold' is not gold at all but copper for which they had been searching in South America.

By the end of June Ransome had completed the first draft of *Pigeon Post* and read it through: 'AWFUL. No grip anywhere. Masses of corroborating detail needed.' A couple of days later he dismissed his efforts with: 'The whole book is somehow not there. No drama...and worse a development of undramatic bits...no tension...' The story was abandoned for twelve months.

In the meantime, the Ransomes had become restless and decided to leave Low Ludderburn. The damp lakeland climate did not suit Evgenia, and they still longed to buy a yacht in which they could cruise. Life at Low Ludderburn had never been easy without mains water and electricity and it was too remote from the shops. An expedition to Windermere involved a round trip of twelve miles. Evgenia began studying maps of suitable locations and settled on somewhere on the peninsular between the rivers Stour and Orwell and close to the yachting centres at Pin Mill and Harwich in East Anglia. Eventually, they rented Broke Farm on the northern side of the River Orwell, which was as near as they could find at the time.

Before leaving the lake, Ransome put *Swallow* up for sale — a move he could not have contemplated a couple of years previously when *Swallow* was the apple of his eye. She had been put in the care of George Walker's boatyard at Bowness and moored to a wooden buoy proudly bearing her name. Ransome had fallen out of love with the boat because she was too slow. He had suffered an embarrassing defeat while racing her against Coch-y-bonddhu and being beaten by the length of Belle Isle.

Cocky, as the little boat was known, belonged to Charles and Margaret Renold and had been built by the same yard that had constructed Swallow. Ransome kept an eye on her progress and from time to time sent the Renolds news of her progress:

> She is all but finished planking and we have to report that you are in very great luck. How the devil they do it, I don't know, but they have got hold of the most beautiful spruce for the planking...I think you have got a real bargain and we are both full of envy.

Renold preferred fishing to sailing, and so *Cocky* became Ransome's property. He was particularly proud of her seaworthy qualities: 'Raced *Cocky*, but Genia was cold and found her too small and did not enjoy herself. It was a pity we tried it. But the little boat sailed jolly well.' Walker sold *Swallow* to a local teenager, Roger Fothergill, who disposed of the boat shortly after the outbreak of war. Her fate remains unknown.

Early in August 1936 Ransome had ready a version of *Pigeon Post* which he considered fit for Evgenia to read while he went off sailing for the weekend. Her verdict was distinctly promising, for she said that it was not very much worse than the worst of the others and that only three chapters needed a full revision. Otherwise a few minor alterations would see it ready for the printer. Ransome took up the task enthusiastically, and his diary records that in a couple of days he had sorted out seven of the chapters. Ten days later the finished typescript was sent to the publishers.

Most of the sketches for the illustrations were drawn before he had left Low Ludderburn. When it came to drawing people, Ransome liked to have a model or a photograph to copy, and Gnosspelius posed for photographs showing the right way to pan for gold and how to use a blowpipe. Ransome always had a feeling for composition and a feature of *Pigeon Post* is the effective use he makes of trees which frame the picture.

Oscar Gnosspelius, to whom the book is dedicated, was the model for Squashy Hat, the rival prospector. As recently as 1928, Gnosspelius had started a modest copper mining project high up on the Brimfell shoulder of Coniston Old Man. Sadly, the brave attempt to keep the Coniston copper mining tradition alive was abandoned in 1933. The potential yield was too small and the situation too cold and remote to justify further investment. John (Willie) Shaw had laboured faithfully for Gnosspelius in the Brimfell mine, and when Gnosspelius turned his attention to slate, he put Shaw in as working chargehand. Their mine at Horse Crag Level, near the Tilberthwaite road, had been cut through good slate and an underground quarry had been opened. The description of Slater Bob's mine in the story depicts this underground quarry, with Shaw himself immortalised as the old-timer yearning to return to the copper mining of his youth.

The Romans were probably the first to mine in the Coniston fells, but attempts to win minerals from the depths of the mountain began with the establishment of The Company of Mines Royal in the middle of the sixteenth century, and Queen Elizabeth I took ten per cent of the proceeds. Activity reached its peak three hundred years later with the introduction of copper-cladding to pre-

(This page, top)
The great cavern where Slater Bob told the prospectors of the undiscovered gold.
(Ted Alexander)

(Left)
The entrance to Horse Crag Level in 1992. Slater Bob's Mine in Pigeon Post *is a faithful portrait of the quarry.*
(Ted Alexander)

(Opposite)
Somewhere in 'Ransome Country' the latest generation of explorers follow the footsteps of Titty and Roger up the beck as it crosses the Coniston Fells.

vent fouling of sailing ship hulls by marine life. By that time the area was riddled with shafts, some reaching to a depth of almost 400 metres, and the mines employed 600 workmen. W.G. Collingwood described the mines as: '...a little town of sheds, offices, workshops and waterwheels...'. When Ransome came to know Coppermines Valley, the mines were in decline and large-scale mining had ceased. Today there is much at the site to interest the industrial archaeologist, but apart from the Youth Hostel and a few holiday cottages, the scene still resembles the bleak area around the

Perhaps the earliest surviving postcard sent in response to a young enthusiast is this one which was posted on 9th July 1935.

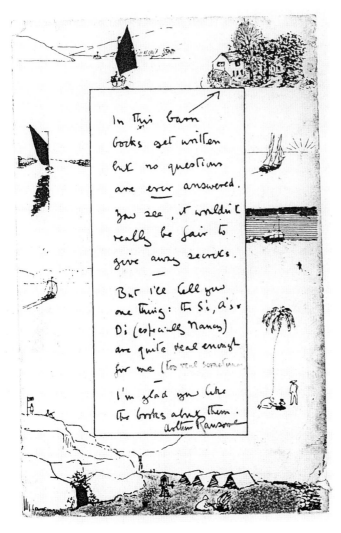

half-way camp to which Nancy sent the Swallows in *Swallowdale*.

The passage through the mountain which was taken by the hurrying moles in *Pigeon Post* really existed. However, reaching the original of Slater Bob's mine from the plateau which Ransome called High Topps involved a complicated expedition down shafts as well as along tunnels. Slater Bob's talk of gold was not completely far-fetched, for some authorities claim that small quantities of gold were found in the Lake District in the Newlands Valley near Keswick.

About ten years ago George Tarr reopened 'Slater Bob's mine' at Horse Crag Level at Tilberthwaite and began quarrying on a small scale using the traditional methods employed by the old miners. Unfortunately the enterprise did not yield sufficient roofing slate to justify working the mine on a more commercial basis.

Until the outbreak of the First World War quarrymen who spent their working week living in tents high on Honister Pass sent messages to their families in the valley below by means of carrier pigeons. They also used pigeons to carry urgent messages to their offices in Keswick. An attempt to employ pigeons in the Coniston quarries was a failure because there were too many hawks in the area. This caused some debate over the title of Ransome's story which, at various stages he called 'Grubbers All', 'Pigeon Post' or 'High Topps' — which was the title Ransome favoured. Wren Howard insisted on *Pigeon Post* and told him to bring the pigeons into the story a little more.

The gold fields themselves, to which Gnossspelius took Ransome, lie beneath Wetherlam and the shoulder of Wetherlam Edge and form part of a whole area known as Above Beck Fells. The upper reaches of the Amazon River are remarkably like that part of Yewdale Beck which lies above Shepherd's Bridge in the Tilberthwaite Valley. Tyson's Farm, the explorers' base, is in a location similar to the farm at Low Tilberthwaite, where a path leads up to Above Beck Fells. The attractive Yew Tree

Farm, alongside the Coniston-Ambleside road fits Ransome's description, and like Tyson's Farm lies beyond a bridge over the beck. Atkinson's Farm, or Ground as it is sometimes called, is merely a name which was borrowed from a farm half a mile up the road from the Collingwood home at Lanehead. Strickland Junction is based on Oxenholme where the branch line to Windermere leads into the hills. It has the overall roof and the stone wall beyond the track that is shown in Ransomes drawing, although the picture has been reversed in order to avoid making the connection too obvious.

By the time Ransome was writing *Pigeon Post*, he was beginning to tire of the letters which were pouring in from fans. Some things amused him, like the box of dates sent by a little girl in California, and the letter from another girl who wrote, 'Please write another book exactly like the last, with the same people, the same places and the same things happening.' So convinced by the portrayal of the Swallows and Amazons was one America mother that she generously invited the characters to spend their summer holidays with her small son. It was the enthusiast who wanted to know too much that irritated Ransome. Among his papers is a very rough handwritten draft of a deterrent which presumably he considered including in future editions:

Scene — The cabin of the houseboat.
Time — about 4 years after publication of the first book about the Swallows and Amazons.
    Nancy is flicking through a great pile of letters on the cabin table.
    Susan is busy at the cooking stove. John is showing Roger how to make an eye-splice at the end of a rope. Titty is writing home. Peggy is looking out of a porthole.
    'Do we do anything about this lot?' asked Nancy. 'He keeps asking us what to say.'
    'Couldn't he just put the letters in the fire?' said John.
    'Lots of them send stamped addressed envelopes,' answered Nancy. 'He says he's got to answer them.'
    'I don't see why,' said Roger. 'Nobody asked them to write.'
    'But there's the stamped envelopes,' said Peggy.
    'He could steam off the stamps and use them for

writing to us at school,' said Roger.
    'He wouldn't do that, anyway.'
    'It's the things they ask,' said Nancy. 'Everyone asks, "Are they real?"'
    'Beastly cheek!' said Roger
    'If I had the time, I'd [illegible] who's real?' said Nancy.
    'And what about the ones who ask him to tell the real names of our best places?' said Peggy.
    'He's said too much already,' said Nancy. ' Look at the way they found out the harbour of Wild Cat Island in spite of his careful moving of the geography!'
    'It was awful finding someone had been at our old harbour and painted the leading mark with white paint. They must have read the book.'
    'We begin to think he ought never to have written the books.'

Even in his correspondence, Ransome's handwriting was not all it might have been. Ivy commented once: 'Thank you for your letter. May I say without offence that your handwriting is improved.' Lascelles Abercrombie wrote: 'Catherine [Lascelles' wife] thanks you extremely for your letter. She enjoyed it very much. She would have enjoyed it still more if she could have read it.'

Pigeon Post was the first book to be awarded the Library Association's Carnegie Medal, instituted to commemorate the centenary of Andrew Carnegie and awarded annually thereafter to the best book for children published during the preceding year. Ransome recalled the ceremony in Scarborough in his *Autobiography*:

> ...it was a very fine day, and a large round medal, and I enjoyed meeting Temple [the Archbishop of York], whom I had last seen shouting with laughter in the quadrangle at Rugby about forty years earlier. He talked very well about detective stories and grew red in the face with indignation as he spoke of one or two constructors of such tales who, in his opinion, did not play fair.

Gratified as he was with this public recognition, Ransome was equally pleased to receive a letter of congratulation which had been signed by the entire staff of Jonathan Cape.

(Above)
The much photographed Yew Tree Farm seems the most likely contender for the origin of Tyson's Farm.

(Right)
Tilberthwaite and Yew Tree Farm from the road to Tarn Hows.

Chapter Eleven
WE DIDN'T MEAN TO GO TO SEA

In September 1935 Ransome bought a 7-ton cutter that he renamed *Nancy Blackett*, saying that if it had not been for the exploits of Nancy and her friends, he would not have been in a position to afford the boat. While Evgenia was packing up and preparing to leave Ludderburn, he sailed from Poole, where *Nancy* had been lying, to Pin Mill, just across the river from their new home.

Nancy left Poole harbour in a gale and was almost swept on to the notorious Shingles Bank. Only the faithful Handybilly engine, which started instantly when called upon, prevented the voyage from ending in disaster. With the help of his strong young crewman, Ransome managed to reach Yarmouth on the Isle of Wight where they learned that the lifeboat had been alerted by the coastguard to rush to their rescue. He wrote in the log: 'Consider the boat pretty good and the engine a real beauty.' Later he confided to Barbara Gnosspelius that sailing round the coast to Pin Mill was much more difficult than cruising in the Baltic.

The sailing season was over before the Ransomes had settled in at Broke Farm, '...a plain red brick house, with the cowsheds and dairy on one side of it and on the other a row of cottages.' From the upper room in which Arthur worked, 'I could see the river and the mouth of Levington Creek, with Harwich harbour and in the distance, Landguard Point and the open sea.'

Life at Levington proved to be quite different to the pastoral existence to which they had become accustomed during the ten years spent in the Lake District. Ransome says in an unpublished part of his *Autobiography*:

Levington brought about a very great change from our hermit-like life at Ludderburn. We were within easy reach of London and I could go up for the day whenever I wanted to chatter, and our friends could run down to chatter with us. Molly Hamilton,...Howard of Cape's, my Mother and my Aunt Helen who delighted in going down to the creek and walking along the sea wall watching the ships. We had, too, a great many web-footed visitors, even in that first winter.

Cocky had been sent down by train and was kept in the nearby creek, ready for sailing across to *Nancy's* mooring on the other side of the river. Each winter *Nancy's* gear was brought home and stored in the attic where he scraped and varnished the spars and greased the rigging — activities which made a useful break from work on books.

Yet not all the changes brought about by the move were pleasant. After living for ten years with nothing to disturb him but the bleating of sheep down in the valley, they now had to contend with near neighbours at Levington:

We were also very much too close to those cottages. In one, just the other side of our wall, there was a child whose pleasure it was to lean out of the window and shout at nobody in particular for hours on end...(This is the child referred to in Lady Kennet's autobiography as 'crying'. It never cried. It got too much enjoyment from merely shouting.)

Ransome was in a buoyant mood in January 1936 when he wrote to Wren Howard that he had the best idea for a new book since *Swallows and Amazons*! After starting the opening chapter,

A drawing from Ransome sketchbook made at Levington. *(Leeds U)*

however, he regretfully put it aside to work on the illustrations that were to replace those by Clifford Webb in a new edition of *Swallowdale*.

The fictional voyage that thrilled him so much seems to have its origin in the real-life North Sea crossing made by the yachting writer, Maurice Griffiths, aboard his wife's yacht *Juanita*. The story of Griffiths' crossing is told in his yachting classic, *The Magic of the Swatchways*, in 1932. *Juanita* drifted out to sea from Harwich Harbour on the ebb tide, past the Beach End buoy where a fog came down and they heard the dismal moaning of the Sunk light-vessel. Griffiths' wife was helplessly sick over the cockpit coaming, and they had a close encounter with a steamer in the dark. Boxes and baskets of flotsam floated by. All these episodes were woven into the story of the Swallows' unsought voyage to Holland. The use of a strong torch and a Woolworth plate to frighten off the Harwich-Hook steamer in Ransome's story came from his recent voyage from Poole to Pin Mill, when *Nancy's* navigation lights kept blowing out.

In June, after a few short trips in *Nancy* that

Ransome had not thought worthy of entry in the log, he set sail for Holland to check on every aspect of the voyage and local details. Finding *Nancy's* galley beside the companion steps too cramped, Evgenia was unwilling to make the trip. So Ransome took someone that he hardly knew. They were barely out of the harbour before the man urged him to give up the idea of crossing the North Sea. The weather forecast promised light westerly winds, but by nightfall the man again wanted them to turn back for the coast. Ransome insisted on completing the crossing, but when they finally tied up in Flushing, he had been at the helm for most of the passage, and his mate had shown himself to be next to useless.

To add insult to injury, when they went ashore and made the acquaintance of the local pilot, the man tried to pass himself off as a professional seaman from sailing ships! Ransome paid his fare and saw him off on the Harwich ferry, 'heartily glad to

(Above)
Nancy Blackett *in Chichester*
Harbour in 1998.

(Left)
Broke Farm
(Ted Alexander)

(Above)
Tony Ward, the Pin Mill harbourmaster, sets out from the hard in the old style, preferring oars to outboards, on his way to replace one of the mooring buoys.

(Right)
The windows of Alma Cottage still look out on 'a place where land in comparison with water, seemed hardly to matter at all.'

see the last of him.' After several days of head winds which kept *Nancy* from leaving Flushing, Ransome took on a young Dutchman, who had been recommended by the pilot, and returned to Pin Mill after a very pleasant voyage that made amends for the first crossing.

Ransome was always able to weave his own experiences into his stories and on her return from Flushing *Nancy Blackett* met the four-masted barque *Pommern* towing out of Ipswich. In the story *Goblin* meets the giant grain-racer and Commander Walker, who knew about the last surviving deep-water fleet of commercial sail, told the Swallows about the shipowner Gustaf Erikson and the harbour at Mariehamn in the Aland Islands, where today the *Pommern* is still afloat as a museum ship.

That summer the attractions of being afloat proved too great, and it was not until *Nancy* was back on her mud berth, and her gear had been brought ashore for the winter, that Ransome began to write the 'sea book' in which she was to star as the *Goblin*. The story opened on the day following the fire on High Topps, when a telegram brought the news that Commander Walker was making his way home from China and the four Swallows were to join Mrs Walker and Bridget and stay at lodgings in Pin Mill. When he came to revise the first chapter, Ransome decided that the story should start with the Swallows aboard a borrowed dinghy at Pin Mill, having arrived only the day before.

The Swallows befriend Jim Brading, a young man sailing his red-sailed cutter single-handed and they are allowed to spend a few days aboard on condition that they do not venture outside Harwich harbour. Early one morning, with the Swallows aboard the *Goblin* as it lies anchored near the harbour mouth, Jim rows ashore for petrol. As the morning passes Jim fails to return and it becomes foggy. When the anchor fails to hold the *Goblin* on a rising tide, they find themselves drifting blindly out to sea. The weather worsens and they find that there is no alternative but to sail onwards — towards Holland. Arriving in Flushing, after surviving a ferocious gale and having taken a pilot aboard, they are spotted by their father who is just in time to make a pierhead jump from a departing steamer. Reunited, they sail happily back to England. The story tells how the Swallows, faced with a life and death situation, respond in their different ways to a test of their courage, family unity — and in John's case — to his seamanship.

The geography of the story is authentic, and for the first time living people were introduced under their own names. Annie Powell actually lived at Alma Cottage and Frank Adams was the rigger at Harry King's boatyard at Pin Mill. In those days Alma Cottage was an L-shaped building which has since been divided into three cottages, Seagulls, Riverside Cottage and Alma Cottage. The portrait of Pin Mill, with seventeenth-century waterside inn and its barges and anchored yachts, is particularly satisfying. Barges resting high, but as Roger observed, 'not exactly dry', on the hard were an important feature of 'this happy place where almost everybody wore sea-boots, and land, in comparison with water, seemed hardly to matter at all.' The barges have now almost entirely deserted Pin Mill and the spot has lost something of its special character as a result, although the annual Pin Mill barge race is still held. Most of the surviving barges can be found at the Essex town of Maldon and at St Katherine's Dock in London, both of which are more convenient for charter work and business entertaining.

The most likely model for Jim Brading was Jim Clay, who was about to go up to Oxford when he first met Ransome in 1935. The book is dedicated to his mother, Mrs Henry Clay, whose husband had been a colleague of Ransome's on the *Manchester Guardian*. The original idea almost certainly came from the Clay family who had made a North Sea crossing themselves. Another possible candidate was Dick Tyzard, a Rugby pupil and Clay's contemporary at Oxford, who occasionally crewed aboard *Nancy*.

By the middle of the following June the first draft was complete. Ransome left Evgenia to read the manuscript while he sailed down to Brightlingsea. Arriving home after an exhilarating but tiring sail, he was in no fit state to be told Evgenia's verdict, which was typically blunt and to the point. 'Flat, not interesting, not amusing, no dialogue, skeleton only...' Ransome unwisely asked if there was any good chapter. The answer was a firm, 'No.' A few days later the typewriter was busy again and he began the second draft. 'My own book goes grimly on. I have found a few good spots in it, in spite of the condemnation of the critic on the hearth.'

Apart from his work on *We Didn't Mean to Go to Sea* that summer, he took pleasure in playing godfather to *The Far-Distant Oxus*, a highly original book in the Ransome tradition which had been written by two schoolgirls, aged fifteen and sixteen. He was hugely impressed by the manuscript that Katharine Hull and Pamela Whitlock sent him of a story they had written in secret whilst at boarding school. Jonathan Cape agreed to publish the book if Ransome would write an introduction. On Ransome's insistence, Cape merely corrected the spellings and allowed the book to emerge as fresh as when the girls had written it, triumphantly justifying their claim: 'By children, about children, and for children.'

Ransome enjoyed the occasional game of squash, chess or billiards, and he rarely missed an opportunity to sail *Nancy Blackett* down the river.

The Loom of the Lighthouse illustration for We Didn't Mean to Go to Sea.

Evgenia was still less than enthusiastic about *Nancy*, but whenever they sailed together they worked admirably as a team. One entry in the log speaks eloquently of their working relationship afloat:

> 11.20 called on deck, to find that Genia had decided to pass Cork Spit (buoy) on the wrong side, and, pinching to get to windward of it, was in irons, without steerage way, ten yards from it, being carried straight on it. Crashed. Fended off as best could with a boathook, but pretty useless. Poor Genia very much upset. However, it 'might have happened to anyone, and tides are damned deceptive things.' Continued and had a good sail...

At the beginning of September Ransome sent the second draft of *We Didn't Mean to Go to Sea* to Wren Howard. '...I am very dissatisfied with parts of it. Still, I am prepared to accept your verdict. If you think it doesn't need such wholesale alteration as would take a very long time, I will do what I can with it at once. If on the other hand you think it's in such a hopeless mess that it would take months to put right, why then I'll sit on it a bit, go off for a holiday, and rewrite it during the win-

ter.' Wren Howard's verdict was favourable: 'I do honestly think very well of the book indeed. It gathers pace in a most satisfactory manner and works up through the crises to an admirable conclusion.' When Evgenia read it for the second time, she was full of praise. Ransome noted in his diary: 'Genia says book does not need much doing to it. So it will get done this year after all.'

Wren Howard thought that Jim's accident should not be revealed until the end of the book, and that the quiet chapter with Mother and Bridget at Pin Mill was excellent and made the break in just the right place. Ransome took his advice: 'The hospital nurse chapter is OUT, and I've left Jim wandering around the room, finding the card with "Talks English" on it...to his indignation, in the chapter about his waking up at the end of the book. Account of accident simply left to the bus conductor in the same chapter. I fear a lot of people will say the thing's too tough for babes.'

When not busy revising, Ransome was hard at work on the pictures. He was not happy with the results in spite of the detailed sketches he had made aboard *Nancy* and the photographs he had taken at Flushing. 'With the exception of the lightship and Pin Mill, the drawings horrify me by their badness. One howling bit of dreadful drawing after another.'

Finally, Ransome parted gloomily with the finished typescript: 'I do wish it was a better book,' he wrote. Wren Howard was unequivocal: 'I spent a delicious day with it on Saturday, and am now writing to thank you for the pleasure it gave me. I think in many ways it is the best of the lot, and I shall never believe another word you say about your own books. It won't be any use your telling us that your next manuscript is hopeless; we just shan't take any notice.' There are many readers

who would agree with Wren Howard's assessment.

Ransome's verdict on the illustrations was not shared by John Masefield, to whom he sent a copy of the finished book. The two had been friends since they met in Edwardian London. Masefield replied:

> So many thanks for your charming kind letter and the gift of your two books: both of them new to me and very delightful.
>
> You are a lot too modest about your illustrations. All sailors can draw ships: and what could be better than your 'Night Encounter' or your tail-pieces of the barges and the shag; and the matchless sketch of the salving of the gear at sea? This is like one of the Marryat drawings, full of life and go! Well done.
>
> I am reading the books with joy and thank you for them.
>
> Yours ever

After publication, Wren Howard had to allow Ransome to redraw the figure of John at the crosstrees for the second impression, but the result was, 'Not much better than the old one but at least it's a boy and not a rather scrawny man.'

J. R. R. Tolkein's book *The Hobbit* was published a few weeks before *We Didn't Mean to Go to Sea*, and Ransome, having spotted a few minor errors, wrote to the author: 'As a humble hobbit-fancier (and one that is certain that your book will be many times reprinted) may I complain that on page 27, when Gandalf calls Bilbo an excitable little hobbit, the scribe (human no doubt) has written 'man' rather than 'hobbit' by mistake?' Tolkein replied: 'I am sure Mr Baggins would agree in words such as he used to Thorin: to have been fancied by you, that is more than any hobbit could have expected.' In the second edition he replaced the word 'man' with 'fellow'.

We Didn't Mean to Go to Sea did extremely well. Almost all the first printing of 12,000 copies had been sold by Christmas. Wren Howard wrote joyfully to Ransome with the news that Selfridges had taken 50 copies and that Harrods and Bumpus, the large Oxford Street bookshop, had each taken 100.

The Swallows and Amazons books were now beginning to reach wider audiences. The BBC

(Top)
Pin Mill with the Butt and Oyster and Alma Cottage.

(Lower)
As recently and the 1970s there were still plenty of barges left high, 'but not exactly dry' on the hard.

began the first of a number of readings with a semi-dramatised version of *Swallows and Amazons* in four episodes. This was followed in 1937 by a much fuller treatment of *Peter Duck* in 17 readings, each lasting twenty minutes. *Winter Holiday* was broadcast in 1941, *Old Peter's Russian Tales* in 1942 and *The Big Six* in 1943. After the war there were broadcasts of *Pigeon Post* and a repeat of *Swallows and Amazons*. All the readings were by Derek McCulloch, and all but one of the adaptations were made by David Davis.

There had been a problem about the number of sailing terms in the Swedish editions of *Swallows and Amazons*. Ransome wrote to Wren Howard:

I believe that the success of the English books has proved that children are prepared to accept and enjoy exact technical detail in such matters as sailing. (Even children in the Middle West of America who have never seen a boat in their lives). I do not believe that there exists a Swedish child who does not know enough about a boat to want to know more, and the whole point of my books is that they do not insult children by assuming that they do not want to use their brains or have no brains to use.

There were now seven books in the series and Ransome became concerned that new readers should begin with one of the early books: 'I think it would be a serious pity if any child were to come FIRST to, say, *Peter Duck* and still more if he or she were to come first to *We Didn't Mean to Go to Sea*.' He tried unsuccessfully to persuade Cape to circulate a note: 'The author particularly asks booksellers not to sell later volumes of these books to any readers who have not read *Swallows and Amazons*, *Swallowdale* or *Winter Holiday*.'

Chapter Twelve
WAR AND PEACE

Ransome decided that his next book should be set on 'muddy creeks...tidal...an island...like Walton backwaters...' His publisher suggested that the story might revolve around Titty and Roger and some new characters from Pin Mill: 'Temporary exclusion of John and Susan would give a new focal point and age level.' Remembering Ransome's outburst at the use of the word teenagers, perhaps he foresaw the difficulty of John and Susan prolonging their childhood after their adventures in *We Didn't Mean to Go to Sea*. Up to a point, Ransome took Wren Howard's advice and excluded the elders from five key chapters of *Secret Water* — the discovery of the hoofmarks, the capture of Bridget, the Red Sea episode and the mapping of the North West Passage.

Yet, in the summer of 1938, Ransome was too preoccupied with the construction of a new and larger yacht to give much thought to the next Swallows and Amazons story. *Selina King* was built in Harry King's yard at Pin Mill, while Ransome haunted the boatyard to gather material for a book he hoped to write about her building. He had promised Evgenia a roomy galley, but, large as it was, she complained that the designer and he between them had cheated her out of six inches.

Meanwhile, apart from a memorable cruise to Portsmouth, *Nancy Blackett* remained in local waters, sailing in the harbour and down the coast to Kirby Creek and Waldringfield. After the North Sea episode no more paid hands were taken aboard but there were always friends willing to crew for him, notably Philip Rouse, whom he had chanced to meet while fishing. It had been their first encounter since attending Rugby together. During the school holidays Ransome was able to call upon the services of more youthful crews:

> One day...I had come sailing into Levington Creek in *Cocky* and saw a boy and girl running along the sea wall. They were waiting by the sluice as I brought the boat in and made themselves very useful. Those two, George (killed at El Alamein) and Josephine, were the children of the Russells who were renting Broke Hall from the same landlord from whom we were renting Broke Farm. They became much valued allies. Both had a natural genius for small boats and whenever G. was too busy with her garden to come to sea with me and *Nancy*, George and Josephine, if not at school, could be counted on. Moored not far from *Nancy* at Pin Mill was an eight-ton cutter *Lapwing* belonging to Col. Busk, and sailed by him as a family boat. Busk and I were to sail much together, and his family joined in our various ploys.

Sailing with young people brought out the best in Ransome. Josephine Russell, who was younger than her brother and accustomed to being put down, was astonished to find Ransome a very patient teacher who treated both of them alike. Even after 15-year-old Jill Busk put *Selina King* on the mud near Ipswich there were no recriminations. When the Russell youngsters wanted a boat of their own, Ransome lent them *Cocky* and had another *Swallow* dinghy built for himself.

The Ransomes' Broads holidays took the form of large-scale expeditions in which they led a fleet of identical *Fairways* crewed by their young sailing friends.

The average age of the skippers in charge was extremely youthful, and most of them were very effi-

(This page, top) 'Muddy creeks...tidal...an island...like Walton backwaters...'

(Left) Selina King *has cruised extensively in the Caribbean. The vessel is seen here after restoration in Bermuda in 1999.*
(Hal White)

(Opposite, top)
Looking like an inland sea — Twizzle Creek at high water.

(Lower)
The Wade crosses the broad expanse of mud left by the the receding tide and links Swallow (Horsey) Island to the mainland.

Ransome sailing **Coch-y-bonddhu** *at Pin Mill.*
(Josephine Russell)

Colonel Busk and his wife Kathleen with their children John and Gillian aboard **Lapwing.**
(courtesy Gillian Beevor)

cient. It was a condition of coming on this expedition that each boat must have her Jolly Roger, so that in case of separation, we should be able to recognise our allies at a distance. On the Broads, where the waterways are often above the surrounding country, it is possible to see the white sails of boats miles away, and we thought it well to be sure of our boats from others if one of them failed to reach in time for supper the rendezvous we had chosen for the evening.

On September 27th, just as *Selina King* was about to be launched, Ransome wrote the word 'War' in his diary. Two days later he invited all who had worked on the yacht, as well as many of his sailing friends, to a celebration in the Butt and Oyster inn on the river front at Pin Mill. On the following day, Prime Minister Neville Chamberlain returned from talks with the German Fuhrer, Adolf Hitler, to announce 'Peace in Our Time', and Ransome confined his diary entry to just 'Peace'.

Against his clear disinclination to dabble in politics since reporting the revolution in Russia, he told his mother that 'in spite of all that will be said against him, I think Chamberlain has done extremely well'. While reminding her that both the Czechs and Poles had swallowed up bits of neighbouring territory, he went on to say: 'Chamberlain seems to have done right WHAT-EVER the outcome. Because, if after all we do have to fight, we shall have the moral support of the whole world' for at least trying to obtain a just and peaceful settlement of European borders first. In the same letter Ransome commented: 'Selina seems most awfully big. Comfortable to live in but a bit of a handful to sail. However, if war does come, there won't be any sailing.'

Before parting with *Nancy Blackett*, he took George and Josephine aboard for a cruise round the extraordinary landscape of Hamford Water, which lies behind the east coast town of Walton on the Naze. In Kirby Creek they found *Lapwing* at anchor, with the younger members of the Busk family camped nearby on Horsey Island. Busk had made a blank map, and they all set off to explore and fill in the details of the winding maze of sea channels and islands.

In 'Marooned' or 'The Mastodon Boy', as Ransome originally called his new book, the Swallows are left to themselves on Horsey Island in the Walton Backwaters, so allowing Commander and Mrs Walker time to settle in at the Shotley naval establishment. The castaways meet a local boy, who lives on a derelict barge, and another boy and a girl. After some bad weather and an exceptionally high tide, the Swallows drift out to sea on a barely finished raft as their island becomes swamped.

The opening three chapters of what eventually became *Secret Water* were written in December 1938. By the middle of January Ransome had decided that the Swallows needed some sort of objective, rather than simply being cast ashore. Borrowing the Busk's mapping project, he set to work on the chapters where John surveys the island and Titty and Bridget discover the mastodon footprints.

By the spring, with the book well under way, the Ransomes had realised their dream of moving away from their noisy young neighbour to the other side of the river where they rented an isolated farmhouse. Harkstead Hall was just a few minutes drive from Pin Mill and close to the home of the Busks, with whom they remained friends for thirty years. Their young 'pirate' children owned two dinghies, *Wizard* and *Zip*, and by using a borrowed dinghy, *Jo*, they were each able to skipper their own vessel. Ransome wrote of those visits in his *Autobiography*:

> *Selina* was sailing as early as 12th March and we spent a great deal of time in her going again and again to Kirby Creek with the Busks, the Corsons and George and Josephine Russell and others of our young web-footed acquaintances. The King of Horsey Island was now David Haig Thomas, Greenland explorer, who was busy with strange geese there. Queen Nancy, Mrs Haig Thomas, was the daughter of Bury, with whom I had sailed on the Nile, duck-shooting. They used to struggle through the mud to come aboard *Selina*, (taking off their boots in the dinghy out of respect for Selina's well scrubbed decks and spotless cabin), and by letting us have fresh milk they kept my vile corkscrew quiet while I lay at anchor and worked sometimes for days on end.

Secret Water opens with the news that Commander Walker, who had planned to take his family map-making in Hamford Water, has to take up his shore appointment at *HMS Ganges* immediately. Instead, he maroons all five children on Horsey Island with a borrowed dinghy and they begin their own map-making expeditions. The Mastodon Boy befriends them, and the Amazons arrive from the north, but the rest of the Mastodon's tribe of Eels send a message telling him to do everything he can to get rid of the interlopers, short of setting fire to their tents. The Eels were loosely based on the Busk children and the dedication of the book is to the Busk family. With little interest in map-making, Nancy wants to go straight for the enemy's camp and bang an arrow into the middle of their fire, but the others manage to restrain her warrior instincts. The tribe

(Above)
Witch's (Kirby) Quay at low water.

(Right)
The witch's cottage stands a short distance from the quay.

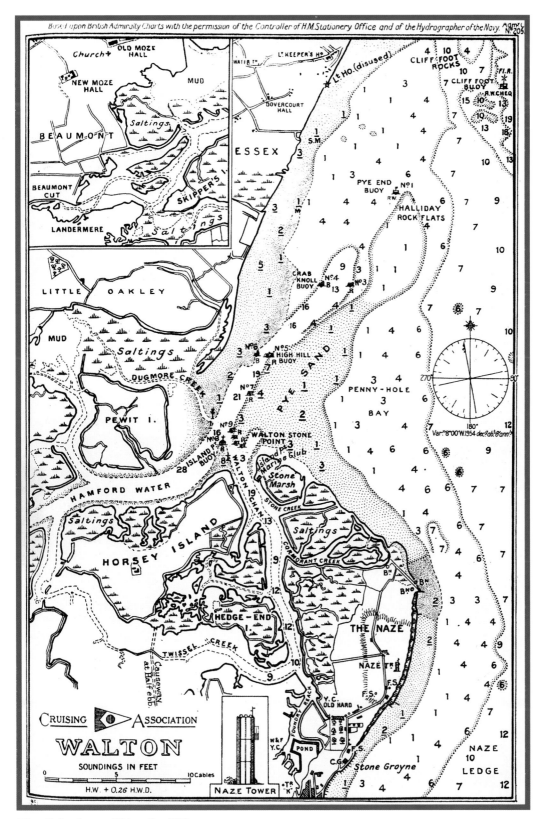

The C.A. chart of Hamford Water (Courtesy of The Cruising Association)

eventually make peace after Bridget, who is taken hostage, explains why they have invaded the Eels' private territory. Nancy finds their leader, Daisy, a kindred spirit, and so with the Mastodon torn between old and new loyalties and Nancy facing the heart-searching question of whether to remain faithful to her old allies, nothing is quite what it seems.

Bridget is now considered old enough for camp life. Her naiveté and determination not to be left out provide some of the story's funniest moments, and the subtlety of Bridget's relationship with Titty and Roger is among the delights of the story.

Apart from an imaginary creek that was invented in order to make Titty's disobedience credible, *Secret Water* gives a satisfying and completely accurate portrait of the lonely marshes. The causeway linking Horsey Island to the mainland is the most striking feature of a place which has changed remarkably little since Ransome's day. It is reached by a lane leading from the B 1034 road to Walton. To pause in the middle of a shining expanse of mud halfway across the wade is an uncanny experience. A short distance away from Kirby Le Soken the world seems to have forgotten the old barge quay and granary at Kirby Quay which Ransome called Witch's Quay. The granary is now a fine marshland home, but otherwise Witch's Quay remains unchanged, and there is a feeling of timelessness about the place. The witch's cottage itself is a holiday home and kept in excellent repair. Those who knew the area in the days before the Second World War are agreed that there was a barge, similar to Speedy, abandoned in the mud off Skippers (Mastodon) Island, and several other barges ended their days somewhere among the backwaters.

Ransome beefed up the ending by giving Titty and Nancy a bad conscience, so that they sail off at the crack of dawn on the morning of departure to complete the map, leaving John, Susan and Bridget to strike camp in time for Commander Walker to take them home.

The drawing of the meal-dial which appeared in the first edition shows the pegs correctly positioned for use in the southern hemisphere. This was put right in later editions, but the fine drawing of the *Goblin* sailing off to Secret Water without *Wizard* in tow was never corrected. Ransome's maps — accurate for their time but not now — almost match the Cruising Association's chart of the period.

Throughout the last, unreal summer of peace, yachtsmen were making the most of every opportunity to be afloat. After the outbreak of war, and with *Secret Water* finally off his hands, Ransome made one of his most remarkable sea passages. At that time all offshore yachting was forbidden, but he had managed, by pulling a few strings, to obtain a permit allowing the 'British Merchant Vessel *Selina King*,' carrying a cargo of 'ballast', to sail up the coast to Lowestoft. In spite of engine trouble and a couple of dangerous landfalls, he brought *Selina King* safely through those troubled waters, avoiding sunken British wrecks and enemy submarines, to reach Oulton Broad where she was put under cover for the duration.

Shortly after the start of hostilitiess Ransome offered his services to the Admiralty but was turned down on the grounds of health and age. He would have nothing to do with the local Home Guard and claimed he had no stomach for the fight. Instead he became Cassandra, predicting doom in his letters to his mother and salvos he fired off to Dick Stokes, the Labour MP for Ipswich. Although he found words of praise for Churchill, he berated the inept moves of Foreign Secretary Halifax and asked: 'How soon shall we call Lloyd George who alone has the courage to speak out.' He blamed Halifax for miscalculating Stalin's intentions and allowing Hitler to fight on one front instead of two, ending a lengthy war homily to his mother by recommending Agatha Christie's detective story *The Murder of Roger Ackroyd*.

Chapter Thirteen
BROADLAND VILLAIN

Once Cape had *Secret Water* safely at the printer, Wren Howard urged Ransome to attend to 'the autobiographical book we want you to write. It would be a major tragedy if it never got written at all.' With the coming of the Second World War, however, Ransome's thoughts had turned to other matters. At the end of September 1939, having laid up *Selina King*, little suspecting that he would never sail her again, he returned to Harkstead with determination to make something of an idea that had been sparked by a gale-torn autumn Broadland cruise two years earlier.

On that occasion the Ransomes had hired a motor cruiser, *Royal Star*, from their friend Jack Powles, who had been hiring out sailing boats to them for years. 'We are neither of us in the least interested in moving about in a motor boat, but we needed a movable houseboat, and we took *Royal Star* from Wroxham and up through Potter Heigham to fish the upper waters of the Thurne...But whatever was wrong with my middle', Ransome later wrote in his long-awaited *Autobiography*, 'was not improved by jumping ashore, mooring or unmooring our cruiser, and so before giving up the boat, back at Wroxham, I called on Dr Bennett.' The good doctor at once dispatched him to the surgeon who, five years earlier, had operated on him for appendicitis. After another successful operation, Ransome suffered an embolism and came close to death. 'You,' said the surgeon with a smile, 'must be a very large-hearted fellow.' Ransome gave all credit to his surgeon who 'had come across the road on the run, I believe in his dressing gown, and somehow or other managed to keep me going.'

When he had fully recovered, he wrote to Margaret Renold, enthusiastically agreeing to her suggestion that he should try a detective story. 'George Owden of Coot Club is obviously the right criminal. Tom and the Death and Glories are the right detectives, with the help of Dorothea's imagination and Dick's scientific mind.' Ransome had already written some episodes prompted by his traumatic holiday — catching the world's whopper, the fisherman and innkeeper, and smoking eels among them. He concluded his letter with a plea for Margaret to come up with a suitable crime for Owden to commit. After *Coot Club*, he reckoned it should not involve visitors' boats:

> It would be all wrong for the detectives to snoop out of public spirit with the hope of handing George over to justice. The detective work must be forced upon them TO CLEAR THEMSELVES of some villainy of which, thanks to George Owden, they are bearing the blame. What the devil can it be?... Gosh, Margaret, if you can provide the right crime, I'll write you the loveliest detective story there ever was.

With no help in the matter from either of the Renolds, Ransome eventually accepted that the crime would have to involve boats. It was already established that Owden was a thief of rare birds' eggs and an enemy of the bird protectors. What could be more natural than that he should plot to have the Coot Club discredited and prevented from enjoying the freedom of the river, so leaving him free to pillage as he wished the following spring? Everyone knew that Tom had cast off the *Margoletta*; if more boats were to be cast off, everybody would jump to the obvious conclusion...

The story was to be set in the autumn (the best

(This page, top) *'A light breeze was stirring the river and they could see water sparkling through the trees.'*

(Left) *This early colour photograph of Horning perfectly captures the atmosphere of* **The Big Six.**
(Blakes)

(Opposite, top)
The dentist's window stood above the slip at Banham's boatyard exactly as it appeared in **The Big Six.**

(Lower)
The Ferry Inn at Horning has been rebuilt twice since Ransome's time. The original inn and the ferry pontoon were destroyed by enemy action in 1941.

Potter Heigham bridge.

time for pike fishing) or just before Christmas, when Ransome thought he could have fun with the *Death and Glory's* stove and it would make the capture of the giant pike more believable. The story contains echoes of the exploits of Frank, Dick and Jimmy in *The Swan and Her Crew* by Christopher Davies, published in 1876, which Ransome had read. The boys build their own very singular boat, have a 'den' for private business, visit eelmen at night and catch a monster pike even larger than the world's whopper.

In spite of the German bombing raids and the knowledge that the authorities could evict them at any time, and requisition Harkstead Hall for military use, Ransome seems to have found the actual writing of the story much less painful than usual. He toyed with titles: 'Coots in Trouble', 'Hot Water', 'Scotland Yard', 'Who the Mischief?' and 'Not Us'. There was a battle royal over the matter after Ransome had settled on *The Big Six* because Wren Howard wanted to call the book 'The Death and Glories'. Ransome was not the easiest of authors and Jonathan Cape advised his partner, 'I

don't agree, but it is useless to argue with A.R. in these matters, so you had better give him his head.' Eventually Ransome had his way, but *The Big Six* must seem obscure to anybody who has not heard of the Metropolitan Police Superintendents who were known as 'The Big Five'.

The first draft was finished by April 1940 and Genia's verdict amounted to high praise. She thought the framework was the best yet, two of the chapters were good and she had laughed several times! 'So I am full of hope,' Ransome wrote to his publisher, 'though very much afraid that Mr Hitler, that illiterate bloke, will butt in before I get the revision typed out.' By the time he was a third of the way through his final version, Ransome was conceding that he was 'getting some fun out of it in spite of the difficulty of concentration.'

It is remarkable that *The Big Six* was published so quickly. Wren Howard was working in a bomb disposal squad all night and in the cellars below the Cape offices all day. The uncertainties of the post added to their problems. Then, at the end of September, came the news that the blockmaker's works had been bombed and the blocks for *The Big Six* (metal impressions from which to print the drawings) were completely destroyed. Fortunately most of the original drawings had already been returned to the publishers who quickly found another blockmaker, while Ransome hastily replaced the few missing drawings. The combination of Ransome's fine illustrations and the crimson he chose for the dust jacket made it the most striking book of the series.

The Death and Glories have been hard at work all summer putting a cabin, three bunks and a stove into their old boat. Ransome found such a boat and drew a careful plan of it. He noted on his drawing that it was 21ft long and 4ft deep. It is the very end of the summer holidays when George Owden begins his nocturnal programme of theft and interference with moored boats in order to discredit the Coots. The Death and Glories proclaim their innocence but, because of their age and social class, almost everybody is prepared to believe the worst. It is hardly surprising that Bill feels some resentment: 'All right for them. Nobody'll turn Tom Dudgeon off the river.' The theme of the story is the most serious in the entire canon; the boys stand accused of crimes that they did not commit and which contravene the code by which they live. The Death and Glories are able to do nothing but await events, although privately Pete continues to hope.:

> Perhaps by now someone had found out who had cast *Sir Garnet* adrift and everything would be all right and there would be no more shouting at the crew of the *Death and Glory* about things they had never even thought of doing...and wouldn't have wanted to do if they had thought of them.

Only with the arrival of the Ds can the Coots begin to respond. It is Dorothea who sets them off: 'Somebody must be doing it on purpose...What we want are detectives.' Under Dorothea's leadership The Big Six begin their search for clues, although her melodramatic asides irritate the more down to earth detectives: '"But there ain't a murder, not yet," said Bill.' Eventually, it is her insight into human behaviour which leads to the formation of a daring plan to catch the villain in the act. They know that if the plan should backfire, nothing can save the Death and Glories. The tension mounts until the very end when the innocent Coots come face-to-face with the villains in front of a lawyer.

Ransome's favourite episodes that had been planned earlier were woven into the story with great skill so that they move the plot along and provide a useful change of pace. The story is much more than a conventional detective yarn and an account in *The Times Literary Supplement* recognised the book's special quality:

> ...But the adventure, though engrossing, is only a small part of a book in which the cry and flight of birds, the smell of water and tarry ropes, and the jargon of men and boys brought up to use their hands and senses are all delightfully plain to us.

Ransome took only minor liberties with Broadland geography. The staithe at Horning is still the centre of the riverside world. Banham's boatyard once stood below the staithe. It gave way to smart riverside dwellings in the early 1970s, but the shed was similar to Jonnatt's in every respect. The successor to Roy's Stores in the village street still caters for the needs of the boat hirers. Stuffed pike are still to be found in a few traditional Broadland pubs, but the pike in The Swan Inn, referred to in *The Big Six*, no longer hangs over the bar. Following complaints from some of the diners that it put them off their meal, it was removed. The 24lb pike, which was caught by a 12-year-old Horning boy, has found a new home in The Museum of the Broads at Stalham.

Until the late 1920s there was a piece of waste ground where Ransome placed the Wilderness, but large-scale maps of the period and old photographs suggest that it was not quite as he described it. Today the area has been completely developed, although the dykes have been retained. There was never an inn near Martham where he placed the Roaring Donkey — a name borrowed from a hotel near Clacton, where the bar is decorated with vintage sporting equipment but there is no monster pike. The World's Whopper was not the largest pike to have been caught on the Broads. Writing in 1930, Arthur Patterson in his book *Through Broadland by Sail and Motor*, quotes the largest recorded specimen as a pike that weighed 36 pounds when it was caught in 1873. A fish weighing thirty and a half pounds — the same as the world's whopper — was taken by rod and line somewhere on the Broads (Patterson

(Opposite page, top)
Fishing on the River Thurne close to where the world's whopper was caught.

(Lower)
Albion *is a regular visitor to Horning Staithe.*

This page, top)
The 'first of the big boatsheds' on Horning Reach where Joe saw the villain's torch is now the only one, but it still has a fleet of sailing yachts for hire.

(Right)
The real Roaring Donkey inn sign near Clacton.

***The Death and Glories revealed. The unused
sketch for the illustration of the cabin of their
old boat.*** *(Abbot Hall)*

does not say where) in 1880. It measured 1m 18cm in length. By his calculation, such a fish must have been at least 25 years old at the time.

Records suggest that eels have been caught at eel-setts for over five hundred years. Tom Cable had his sett at Kendal Dyke in the 1930s. He reckoned to fish for five successive nights during the time the moon was on the wane. Wet and windy or particularly dark nights were considered to be

the best conditions. The net was always raised with the ebbing tide and kept in place for five hours. It was lowered again after the first of the flood had washed the rubbish out of the nests. About five years ago a Trust was formed to preserve and manage his old sett which was the sole survivor of the traditional variety. Recently the age-old method of catching eels changed when the fishers began using 'fyke' nets of Dutch origin. These have the advantage that they can be set up and left at various places according to the set of the tide. Smoked eels have always been popular, and standing in the garden of a Horning eel-fisherman's cottage is a large cylinder that was once used for smoking the catch.

From 40 pages of sketches, Ransome produced some of his finest drawings to illustrate *The Big Six*, and they add considerably to the book. Probably because he had chosen to remain faithful to the Broadland setting, he has captured the feeling of the slow-moving rivers, wind pumps and willows. He was no longer producing drawings such as Nancy Blackett might have made. Instead we see the work of a more confident illustrator expressing great feeling for the characters and the setting.

The Big Six presents a portrait of the Broads with great economy and charm:

'The morning mist was heavy on the river and on the sodden fields that lay on either side of it. The fields were below the level of the river and the Death and Glories, marching along the rond that kept the river from overflowing, looked down on feeding cattle and horses whose thick coats were pale with moisture.' By the end of the book, readers have been accepted into the Broadland fraternity: 'There is no need to describe their run down the Bure and up the Thurne. On that cold February morning, they took turns in steering the *Cachalot* and in going into her cabin to sit by the stove and get the tingle out of their ears and noses.'

Chapter Fourteen
DODGING THAT DAMNED HITLER

In May 1940, as German Panzer divisions approached the channel ports, the Admiralty called for a fleet of small self-propelled boats between 30 and 100 feet in length, to stand by should they be needed to go to the aid of the besieged Allied armies in France. Ransome offered *Selina King*, but the yacht was rejected because she had only a small auxiliary engine, enough to get her in and out of harbour. After some 300,000 soldiers had been rescued from the beaches of Dunkirk, he took to regaling his mother with his own and the often eccentric responses of his neighbours to Hitler's threat to invade England. The Ransomes' home was under no less threat from the British military. Twenty-four hours notice was all they could expect should the Army or the RAF need to requisition the property.

While Arthur had not found it difficult to adjust to the disturbed nights as the Blitz intensified, Evgenia, who busied herself in the garden by day, was worn down by the air-raids and sleepless nights. During daylight hours troubling noise was closer at hand. The nearby school became accustomed to Ransome's notes requesting that the children play more quietly as he was trying to work. By the time the Battle of Britain had reached its height, all their sailing friends had departed and life at Harkstead Hall had become intolerable. On 20th September Ransome confided to his mother: 'to my great and delighted astonishment, Genia says that, given a decent house, water supply, indoor sanitation etc., she is prepared to go back to the Lakes.' A fortnight later he joyfully announced: 'Your warning came too late! Your son is once more a lake country landowner.'

For 'an awful price', and with Evgenia's approval, Ransome had acquired The Heald, a stone bungalow standing in 17 acres of woodland a couple of miles south of the Victorian scholar John Ruskin's house, Brantwood, on the road running down the eastern side of Coniston Water. With the bungalow came an adjacent 'cottage' workroom, half a mile of lake shore and a private mooring jetty. 'Lake frontage in these parts is valued in diamonds an inch.'

Although Arthur felt he had returned to home territory — walking distance from his youthful holidays with the Collingwood family at Lanehead, and Collingwood's association with Ruskin, which is still much in evidence to the visiting public at Brantwood — the Ransomes found themselves as isolated at The Heald as they had been at Low Ludderburn. Evgenia was soon fretting over the lack of space and Arthur found himself immobilised by a double rupture. When petrol rationing made it difficult to collect supplies from Coniston village on the other side of the lake, he bought a lightweight motorbike which he called 'The Monster'. Forbidden by his doctor to go rowing on the lake, he taught himself to fish for char under sail in *Coch-y-bonddhu*.

By the turn of the year he had started a new story — an exotic Chinese tale — as a sort of sequel to *Peter Duck*. He wrote steadily for six weeks before suffering from 'writer's block'. Should he be indulging in such a fantasy when all his young fans were asking for another book about Wild Cat Island and one of Nancy's wild schemes? 'My old brain is truly bust and worn out,' Ransome wrote to Charles and Margaret Renold, imploring them to help with the plot. 'It can run to headaches but not yarns.'

He gave himself a fortnight to think of a plot with a lake background before returning to a tale

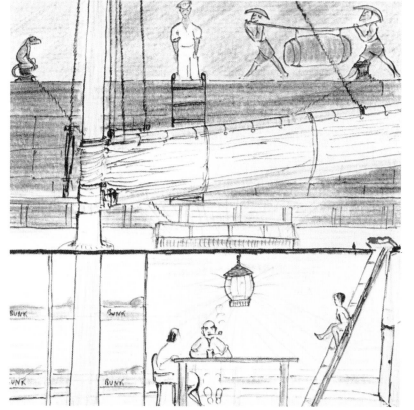

(Above)
The Heald

(Left)
*Ransome's only coloured
sketch for his illustrations is
this unusual cutaway view
for the first chapter of
Missee Lee.*
(Abbot Hall)

he called Poor Miss Lee. Once he was committed to the story he began to badger his friends for background information and Chinese pictures. Before long he had constructed a plot which he spelt out to his confidant, Margaret Renold:

Poor Miss Lee was at Cambridge for about one ecstatic month or term before being called back to China to receive the instructions of her papa, then on his deathbed. He, I may tell you for your PRIVATE information, was a Chinese pirate and at the very top of his profession, for which reason he had done his best to give his daughter (he having no sons) a slap up western education. Now, he dying, she has to give up Cambridge to take charge of his affairs, rule his fleet and territory and keep the pirate business going...I am still much bothered over the intricate girder business of the skeleton which at present it lacks, except for head and tail. Lovely head...elegant tail...but suet pudding in the middle. But that will come right...time is darting on, and Cape's send a howl a week saying they must have the book early, and I am far behind schedule, and that damned Hitler...etc. etc...

Recently Phyllis Hetzel, a Cambridge graduate who would have been a near contemporary of Missee Lee at Newnham College, discovered that in 1935 the daughter of the Chinese politician really had been at Newnham College reading English, so that part of the plot was perfectly feasible.

By the middle of May the first draft was ready for Evgenia to read. Ransome had written the chapters of the early books in the series in sequence, but had since abandoned chronology. After preparing a detailed synopsis, he worked on whichever chapter seemed easiest at the time. This had resulted in inconsistencies in Miss Lee's language, which the 'critic' was quick to point out. In general, however, her verdict was most favourable: 'The critic says the actual skeleton of the book is much better than most of the others.'

The story opens with Captain Flint and his crew of Swallows and Amazons aboard the *Wild Cat* about to leave her hundredth port on a world cruise, bound for Swatow on the nearby coast of China. When the *Wild Cat* is lost by a fire started by Roger's monkey, Gibber, the crew have to take

to their boats and during the night *Swallow* and *Amazon* become separated somewhere in the South China Seas. As daylight dawns they find themselves swept into a colourful and almost timeless world inhabited by pirates whose leader, Taicoon Missee Lee, is a young woman yearning for her lost academic life at Cambridge University. She grabs the chance to detain her English prisoners in order to create her own 'Cambridge' in Dragon Town.

While the captive Swallows and Amazons are waiting to be interviewed by Missee Lee, Nancy assumes command in her most assured manner: 'Look here, John. She's a she-pirate. Let me do the talking.' Soon it appears that Miss Lee is not the pirate chief of Nancy's imaginings, but a Latin scholar who has responded to Roger's cheeky addition to a Latin verse in her dictionary. 'Not Latin,' she tells them, 'that last line, but velly good.' Nancy's put-down is complete when she and Peggy find themselves joined by Captain Flint at the bottom of the Latin class in which Roger has become the established leader. She has one last try to reassert herself: 'Just try Roger in French,' she challenges.

'Flench is not a classical language,' Miss Lee reminds her, and that is the end of the matter.

Eventually, the other leaders of the Three Islands community become suspicious and, in order to save her beloved prisoners' lives, Miss Lee decides to allow them to escape aboard her personal junk on the night of the Dragon Feast. Their flight is soon discovered, but with the Chinese in hot pursuit their only means of reaching the open sea is to attempt a hazardous night-passage through a rock-strewn gorge.

Titty felt about her, found Roger's wrist and held it firmly. She knew. They all knew. For the first time since they had known him, Captain Flint was afraid... 'Can't see,' muttered Captain Flint. ' I can't see....' And then, 'She'll break right up if we touch.... hang on to anything you can and trust to being carried through.... Sorry Susan.... I was wrong.... Thought there'd be more light than this.... I can't do anything with her....'
Roger jerked suddenly. Titty felt somebody stepping over her... soft, silent feet against her body....
'Who's standing?' shouted Captain Flint. 'Lie down,

Studies of floppy hats in Ransome's sketchbook.
(Abbot Hall)

I say. Lie down!'
'Solly. Better let me have tiller, I think,' said the voice of Miss Lee.

What distinguishes the book is the portrayal of the Chinese, the richly conceived setting and its unexpected and satisfying climax.

With such an encouraging verdict from Evgenia, Ransome confidently returned to the book's revision. For a while he considered an alternative ending in which Miss Lee abandons the Three Islands and returns to Cambridge. Wren Howard telegraphed in mid-September: 'Finished proofs midnight stop congratulations twenty-two gong story stop much prefer original ending stop

propose send manuscript to printer stop.'

Ransome had a hard time with the Chinese drawings, lamenting that 'I...can NOT...draw.' He appealed to his friends for suitable pictures. Margaret Renold managed to find some. 'The Chinese pictures are terrific,' Ransome told her and continued, 'I want trees and Chinks...and donkeys...and chopsticks...and opium pipes...sampans...water kongs...costumes...what not.'

Among the 73 pages of Ransome's sketchbook which were devoted to drawings for *Missee Lee* are some accomplished pencil studies of sun hats and figures made by an unnamed artist, quite different from Ransome's vigorous preliminary sketches. When Ransome submitted the finished drawings Wren Howard enthused over them, saying he thought they were 'particularly in tune with the text and really illustrate it.' One of the pictures, however, was to cause Ransome some embarrassment, for a Brownie pack found eight mistakes in Captain Flint's semaphore S.O.S. message. 'Fry, frizzle and broil that fellow Flint,' he wrote to Wren Howard. 'What's the good of my taking trouble, when he goes and lets me down like this?'

Missee Lee is one of Ransome's most complex creations and she provides a glimpse of what he might have gone on to achieve had he not felt compelled to satisfy the demand of fans for more of the Swallows and Amazons when he must have felt the need for a break. He had written five books since he had declared, after completing *Winter Holiday*, that he had finished with the Swallows and Amazons.

The idea of a notorious female pirate inheriting the business from her father seems to have come from *I Sailed with Chinese Pirates* by an American journalist, Aleko E. Lilius. His account tells how the formidable Lai Choi San 'protected' the fishing fleets off Cacao with a fleet of a dozen fully armed junks ready to plunder, kidnap and do battle with rival gangs, even carry out the occasional execution. Ransome said that Missee Lee was inspired by Madame Sun Yat Sen, one the Chinese Nationalist leaders whom he had met in 1927. 'Mrs Sun was born in Shanghai and educated in the Weslyn College in Macon, Galveston, America where she was known for extreme shyness, devotion to her studies, and the difficulty which she found in mathematics.' Missee Lee, it will be remembered, told Captain Flint that he would teach mathematics. Ransome found her 'the most charming little woman, quite young, I suppose well under 30, with an eager expression and eyes that light up easily...'. The other Taicoons, Chang and Wu, are amusing portraits of Chinese warlords Ransome had interviewed.

The hundredth port is most probably Manilla in the Phillipines. During his visit to China Ransome made a voyage up the coast in a small steamship and went ashore at Chefoo, which he described as: 'a little grey and white town surrounded by high brown hills.' Was this the original of Dragon Town? The colourful dragon procession, during which the Swallows and Amazons make their escape, had its origin in the festival he had seen on the streets of Hankow at the time of the Chinese New Year.

A terrific rhythmic gong-beating in the street brings him [the dragon] out of doors. A crowd of men and boys with paper lanterns, gay by day and still gayer at night, precede a dragon borne aloft on poles by twenty or thirty men at regular intervals along its snake-like length. It has a huge carved head painted red, blue, yellow and white, with loose goggling, swaying eyes. Its body is a long tube enclosing at intervals barrel-shaped lanterns. It ends in a carved tail, desperately waggled by a skilful bearer. Immediately before it marches a juggler, swaying two lanterns at the end of ropes, round and round and in and out like Indian clubs, twirling and dancing as he goes. The whole procession is surrounded by gong-beaters, cymbal-bangers, rattlers of split bamboo sticks and splendid spendthrifts of firecrackers.

Ransome had always hoped that his first sea adventure, *Peter Duck* would attract the attention of a film-maker who would want to turn it into a feature film. For a while he also toyed with the idea of commissioning a dramatised version of *Missee Lee*. He asked A.A. Milne, who had written a very successful play based on *The Wind in the Willows*, if he would do the same for *Missee Lee*. Milne saw the task as impossible because of the conflict between what he described as 'real children and cardboard pirates'. Furthermore, he considered that children alone could not carry any play, and Chinese characters speaking in pidgin English would be unable to bring *Missee Lee* to life either. Milne closed with an astute observation on Ransome's appeal: 'What makes *Robinson Crusoe* such an absorbing book is Defoe's absorption in the practical details of how things work. This, if I may say so, is your shining quality and, I suspect, the quality which attracts your readers. But it is not a dramatic quality.'

Missee Lee is dedicated to Ransome's friend Herbert Hanson whose illustrated cautionary Latin rhyme in the front of *The Cruising Association Handbook* was found inscribed in Missee Lee's precious Latin dictionary.

Chapter Fifteen
HIDE AND SEEK

Ransome confidently told his publisher that once he was settled at The Heald he would be writing 'a fresh lot of lake country Swallows and Amazons'. He had already confided his first tentative thoughts to the Renolds:

Subject...I think the Great Aunt of *Swallowdale*. Captain Flint takes Mrs Blackett off for a jaunt abroad, leaving Nancy and Peggy in charge of Beckfoot...Damned good for them. The G.A., hearing this, writes a letter to them refraining from giving her opinion of their mother but making it very plain, and invites herself to Beckfoot to look after them...

In the event, he added just the one further lakeland adventure to the series. It is likely that the framework was suggested by Ransome's Aunt Helen, to whom *The Picts and the Martyrs* is dedicated. Another story, which opened on the Norfolk Broads, foundered when the action reached the lake in the north and was never completed.

Perhaps Ransome wondered how much longer Nancy and Peggy could sustain their roles as Amazon pirates, for he had accepted that Nancy must now be fifteen. Nevertheless in the story the Amazons are still painting Jolly Rogers and calling their neighbours 'natives' before their piracy has to be put aside for a while in order to save their mother from the wrath of the Great Aunt. Brief references to camping on Wild Cat Island and gold mining expeditions in the hills serve only to link the story to the earlier books and to anticipate the freedom they will again enjoy after the Great Aunt's departure.

Unknown to their uninvited guest, the Amazons have Dick and Dorothea staying with them at Beckfoot. Nancy, fearful of the Great Aunt's reaction to what she would regard as parental negligence, ships the Ds off to a nearby hut in the woods in the hope that they can remain there in secret until it is safe for them to return. There are several gloriously funny moments as, one by one, Nancy involves half the neighbourhood in her grand scheme to keep the Ds existence a secret.

To complicate matters, the Ds have a new boat and Dick has been looking forward to helping Timothy analyse some copper samples aboard Captain Flint's houseboat. *Scarab*, the new dinghy, was based on Ransome's own *Coch-y-bonddhu*. The name was probably chosen because a coch-y-bonddhu trout fly is thought to appear to be a swimming beetle. The boatbuilder is not quite ready when the Ds arrive and Nancy utters Ransome's heartfelt observation, based on his experiences with *Racundra* and *Selina King*, that '...the only boatbuilder who ever finished a boat on time was Noah'? When Dick has to 'burgle' Beckfoot in order to fetch some items needed by Timothy for his experiments he is nearly caught by the Great Aunt. Police enquiries follow, but the

(Above)
Windermere on a sunny August morning, is just as it appears in **The Picts and the Martyrs.**

(Lower)
Scarab *was built in one of these Victorian wooden boatsheds that gave character to Bowness Bay before they were pulled down in the early 1970s.*

tables are turned when the Great Aunt goes missing less then twenty-four hours before she is due to leave, and becomes the object of a large-scale hunt. The one thing which must not be allowed to happen is for the old lady to meet the Ds, and so they are sent into hiding aboard Captain Flint's houseboat. Eventually the Great Aunt turns up at Beckfoot having summoned a lift with the Ds and it seems as though Nancy's plan must end in failure.

The first draft of the story was begun early in 1942 and by the end of February had 'reached page 232 in the rough squish...But what squish. Still it's got to be done somehow for export, even if it gets too hectic here and publishers give up and leave the field to the BBC...' In June he reported to Wren Howard:

> Position today: first rough draft completed and ghastly. First 100 pages of second draft now typewritten and rather less ghastly. Total length will be as near as nothing 350 pages of my usual typewriting...Usual 20 full page pictures, I suppose. That means a book slightly, though not a lot, shorter than *Missee Lee*.
>
> I am making Dick and Dorothea the main thread, as in *Winter Holiday*, with Nancy working away as the motive force of the messes, seen mostly through their eyes, and the Great Aunt herself looming in the background, seen by the Ds mostly through the eyes of Nancy, that is to say two degrees removed... until just before the final climax. It is a devilish job and is taking a long time to do. It is the sort of thing that simply can't be rushed...

The revision was ready for Evgenia to read in August while Ransome travelled south for a couple of days spent fishing. When he called at the Cape office on his return, he found an extraordinary letter from Evgenia calculated to overwhelm the good opinion Wren Howard or anybody else might have to offer. She said that the story was 'hopeless', the plot was a pale imitation of what had happened before and even his most faithful readers would find it dull, whereas his rivals would be very happy to see him publish a book that might damage his reputation.

By 1942 there were several successful writers using what might be called the Ransome formula — children having holiday adventures free from

their parents, but enjoying the support of a benevolent uncle-figure and taking place in a recognisable part of the country. In 1936 Jonathan Cape had published the first of Mary Atkinson's Lockett books, *August Adventure*, which was set in Dorset. Further titles were added at the rate of one a year until the series closed with the fourteenth story in 1949. In the case of the three Lockett children and their friends, the adults involved in their adventures were hospitable maiden aunts.

The role of 'Captain Flint' in Aubrey de Selincourt's series of nautical adventures was shared by the artistic Uncle Lance and a 'sort of distant cousin' called 'The Bosun'. *Family Afloat* appeared in 1941 and was followed swiftly by *Three Green Bottles* and *One Good Tern* two years later. Garry Hogg's popular 'Explorer' books told how four children and their intrepid Uncle Guy tour the West Country on tandems, explore Hadrian's Wall on foot and go cruising on the inland waterways in a motor boat. In 1942 the first of David Severn's 'Crusoe' books, *Rick Afire*, was published. Four children discover a mysterious stranger camping in a wood and they befriend him when he is accused by the local farmers of setting fire to a hayrick. They call him 'Crusoe' because his name is Robinson and he becomes their companion in a series of holiday adventures. The closest of Ransome's imitators was Gilbert Hackforth-Jones whose four Green Sailors have a naval officer father. Their sailing exploits with Uncle George and his parrot Polly aboard *Rag Doll* are told with great attention to the practical business of boat-handling. Yet none of these writers retain Ransome's continuing popularity today.

Evgenia's diatribe was enough to prevent *The Picts and the Martyrs* from being published in time for Christmas 1942. Nevertheless, as soon as he was able, Ransome shared his thoughts with Margaret Renold, as he had done many times in the past:

> I feel as if with much thought and trouble I had built a motor car, and painted and varnished it all pretty, only to find that it wouldn't move and never could.
>
> And the maddening thing is that I can't pretend to myself that Genia's wrong. She's right.

In spite of Evgenia's insistence that the story was

beyond redemption, Ransome continued its revision, but he failed to notice that Aunt Maria admonished her great niece Ruth with her piratical nickname 'Nancy' three times in quick succession. The error was quickly corrected and 'Ruth' appeared in later editions. Ransome showed the story to his mother in its revised form, and her good opinion gave him the support he needed to send it to his publisher. Ransome told her: 'One of the partners rushed off to the room of the other with "We've got the Ransome manuscript!" "God bless his mother" was the reply.' Wren Howard and Jonathan Cape liked the book and allocated paper for 25,000 copies. They were remarkably successful in obtaining paper at that period, for most of the books in the series were reprinted eight times during the years of wartime rationing

The Picts and the Martyrs was published in June 1943 and reprinted the following January. Seven years had passed and four books had been added to the series since *Pigeon Post* had appeared in 1936, and his host of readers welcomed a return to the familiar lake country.

The story centres around the hut in the woods called The Dogs' Home. The simple stone building stands beside a path leading into Grizedale Forest to the north of The Heald. It is situated exactly as Ransome described, in a clearing a short distance above the beck where Dorothea does the washing up. The single room with no glass in its window and its door tied up with string — just as in the book — is one of the most satisfying of the Ransome places for the literary explorer to come upon. The high ridge on the Beckfoot promontory from which the Ds spy on the Great Aunt resembles the headland of Holme Crag half a mile south of Waterhead steamer pier on Windermere or the similarly shaped rocky eminence of Watbarrow Point at Wray on the western shore.

Janet Adam-Smith, reviewing *The Picts and the Martyrs* for the *Spectator*, wondered whether 'Mr Ransome's stories appeal to children who live entirely outside the world of nannies, cooks and private boathouses? Or may the line between Ransome readers and non-readers be drawn between town and country minded children...?' Mary Fletcher, a school librarian from Shrewsbury responded with a letter that appeared in the Spectator shortly afterwards. She wrote to say that

Ransome's books were popular with girls of all types and ages and were 'read so vigorously that they have to be replaced or rebound more often then the books of other authors.' Ransome was most gratified:

My publishers sent me a cutting of your very gallant letter to the Spectator in answer to what I think must have been a complaint that my books can only be enjoyed by children of the rich....I should like to point out to the reviewer that it is cheaper to take lodgings in a farmhouse than to take lodgings in Blackpool, that boats are much cheaper than, for example, motor bicycles, that books cost less than legs of mutton and last longer, and that the children in my books are the children of naval officers, boatbuilders' workmen, doctors, farmers, teachers, etc. Also, of course one might ask if the reviewer really thinks that none but birds can read Hans Andersen's 'Ugly Duckling' and that it is necessary to be of the blood royal to enjoy *Hamlet, Prince of Denmark*.

I should be very sorry indeed to think that only children of one particular background can share the fun of doing open air doings, and the feelings that have been common to all young human beings from the beginning of time...It is a great pleasure to me to know that my books are liked in such a school as yours.

Ransome's return to his favourite fishing haunts in the north country rekindled his interest in an idea which had first attracted him while he was writing *Swallowdale*. It was an historical novel celebrating the life of the water bailiff on one of his favourite rivers — the Bela. He described it as a book about 'an old schoolmaster and a fisherman and a boy and a river'. The proposal appealed to his publishers, who offered to commission illustrations from the distinguished artist Charles Tunnicliffe. For a while, during the spring of 1943, Ransome devoted his attention to the Victorian tale which he planned as a celebration of country life and traditional values. He sketched out 31 chapters and had written eight of them before he stopped, never to finish the book. Perhaps ill-health, as well as Evgenia's condemnation of *The Picts and the Martyrs* and her continued opposition to a diversion which she had never liked, proved too much for him. 'God knows I am

(**Opposite page, top**)
There is still a good covering of waterlilies in Octopus Lagoon.

(**Lower, left**) *The path that leads explorers into the world of* **The Picts and the Martyrs.**

(**Lower, right**) *Ransome's illustration was drawn from about the same spot.*

(**This page, top**) *Throughout the story, the Picts and Martyrs are waiting for the return of Mrs Blackett so that they can once again camp on Wild Cat Island.*

(**Right**) *The Dogs' Home is kept just as it was in the story with its door tied in a bow and a window without glass.*

going to need a bit of encouragement'. he wrote to his mother, 'if in spite of local veto, I am going to write any more.' Two superb extracts from 'The River Comes First' were eventually published in 1988 in the *Coots in the North* collection.

Tom is about twelve and his friend Jenny, who is four years younger, have become trapped on an island in the middle of the river after a cloudburst.

...Then we saw it. A wall of water, from bank to bank of the river coming down above the ford. A foot high, it may have been, maybe two feet high, but it seemed more than that to me, and it was over the ford and at us before we had hardly stirred. A wall of water, bubbling at the foot of it, it came roaring down on us. We'd no more time than to get to the high part of the island, and that was none so high, before it was past us and roaring away round the bend below us. Where we had been sitting was two feet of water in a moment, and rising fast. I could see it climbing the banks. There was never a sign of the ford, not a ripple of it, just a great sheet of fast water as far up the river as we could see...I knew there was no time to lose.

'Jenny,' I said, nay, shouted. 'I'm going to get you out of this. But you'll have to bide your lonesome whiles I get across and back again.'

She heard me. I felt her grip my hand, and I saw she was frighted now. There was a tear on her cheek. She was a little lass then, and I was leaving her in the waters with the island going from under her. It was no wonder she was frighted. But she said never a word, and I told her to stay where she was, and I off with my coat and would off with my breeches too, but I knew I'd be wanting a knife, and mine was a big one. I'd have lost it for sure if I'd tried to swim with it in my mouth...lost it or drowned trying to keep it.

After abandoning the Victorian tale, Ransome turned his attention once more to his young Broadland heroes, the Death and Glories. He wrote the first four chapters of a story in which Joe tricks his mates, Bill and Pete into stowing away aboard a motor boat which has been built in Horning but is about to be delivered by road to 'the lake in the north'. After a series of narrow scrapes they arrive in Rio, where they know Dick and Dorothea are on holiday. The boys are stranded, but the boat's owner befriends them and lends them a dinghy. Finally they meet the Swallows, Amazons and Ds sailing on the lake. At this point the narrative ends, but Ransome's few notes and brief synopsis give some idea how he saw the story progressing. Nancy and the others insist that the Death and Glories stay for a holiday, the motor cruiser threads its way throughout the tale, Professor Callum (the Ds' father) is taught to sail and the houseboat becomes the parent ship in a fishing fleet. The story ends with the Death and Glories in command as *Swallow*, *Amazon* and *Scarab*, working together, are able to save Captain Flint's houseboat from blowing ashore after her mooring chain has parted in a gale.

Had Ransome persevered with the story, he might have written a worthy conclusion to the series. As it was, shortly after the Allies had landed in Normandy in June 1944, he received a ready-made plot for a completely different story, and the unfinished Swallows and Amazons adventure had to wait more than forty years before the draft chapters were published as the title story in *Coots in the North*. Some word of the project must have leaked out as an enthusiast wrote to Jonathan Cape as late as 1962 to enquire whether 'More About the Big Six' had been published yet.

Chapter Sixteen
VENTURING MILES NORTH

In a long letter written towards the end of June 1944, Major Myles North congratulated Ransome on his storytelling gifts and showed how intimately he had grown to understand the Swallows and Amazons by spelling out in detail a suggested plot for a new story. The idea involved a rare bird, not known to breed in the British Isles — the great northern diver, which looks similar to its Scottish cousin, the black-throated diver — and a villainous egg-collector. North was a serious ornithologist based in East Africa where he worked for the Colonial Service. He was also an astute literary critic: '...given any set of circumstances the reader knows just how Nancy or Roger or Susan would feel; they are real people and nice lively ones at that...I'd be inclined to compare your way [of writing] with Buchan's and Conan Doyle's, both of whom, to my mind, do it very simply and with great charm.' North's letter did the trick for Ransome, restoring his confidence and enthusiasm. He replied with heartfelt thanks and a number of questions on breeding habits, nesting times and the technicalities of egg-blowing. By August he had abandoned *Coots in the North* and started work on the new book.

At that time, the Ransomes had begun to consider selling The Heald. Arthur hankered to be back on the East Coast, where he could return to sailing once hostilities ceased, and Evgenia longed to leave the damp lake country climate. Over a handshake, upon a chance meeting in a Windermere hotel restaurant, Evgenia agreed to sell The Heald to a Mr Hunter as soon as the war was over for the sum they had paid for it.

In December, Arthur's mother died, and for a while he contemplated buying her house in Kew,

only to be put off by his sister Joyce. After Christmas he wrote to tell her that he was up to page 290 of the 'dullest ditchwater I have ever produced. High time I retired and took to writing sonnets.' In the event, he did not give up on *Great Northern?* The following May he stayed at a fishing lodge near Uig on the island of Lewis — in need, as he wrote to Margaret Renold, of a 'squint at the Hebrides to check the details, which are probably all wrong.'

With the war in Europe at an end, the Ransomes moved out of The Heald in June 1945 and spent six weeks at the Scale Hill Hotel at Loweswater, where some steady work was put into the story. In August they stayed at Jonathan Cape's London flat, a few doors away from the Cape offices in Bedford Square, while they searched for somewhere to live. At first they looked for property near a creek or harbour where *Selina King* could be moored, but Evgenia was unable to find anywhere that pleased her on the East Coast. Eventually they settled on a flat with a large workroom in Weymouth Street, near the BBC. Ransome told his sister of the agent's remark that 'more important than the rent was the tenant.'

> I said nowt on this, but merely gave them references and had got as far as saying that 'if they wanted to know who I was...' when the senior partner at the other end of the room suddenly butted in, and said: 'We know very well who you are. My children have talked of you for years as one of the family, and we are advising the owners to let you have the flat.' ...I think Genia is really pleased.

Having been advised by his doctor to replace *Selina King* with a smaller boat that would be less physi-

(This page, above)
*Port Bun a' Ghlinne — one of
the few possible inspirations
for Scrubbers' Cove with 'the
head' in the distance.*

(Left)
*A 'queer low cottage' or black
house of the Gaels.*
(Ted Alexander)

(Opposite page, top)
*Stornoway Castle overlooks
the harbour where the
Pterodactyl and Sea Bear
were moored.*

(Lower)
*Port Bun a' Ghlinne with its
miniature double bay, Gull
Cliff and Pict-house Hill.*
(David Allcock)

cally demanding, Ransome approached Jack Laurent Giles, one of the leading designers of his day, and asked if he could provide him with a 'ketch-rigged bath-chair'. Numerous letters and plans were exchanged until, early in 1946, Ransome visited Pin Mill where the new boat was being built at Harry King's boatyard. There he was horrified to find that Giles had not given him the headroom he expected. The yacht had been constructed according to plans he had seen and approved, but this did not appear to matter to Ransome, who instantly took against the boat, as did Evgenia, who failed to find a single redeeming feature in Giles's work.

After fretting for a while, Ransome made up his mind to sell the boat back to Giles and his partner in its unfinished state. That should 'see me clear of this disastrous venture...No more boats. Farewell to Pin Mill.' Hardly had the deal been done than the Ransomes changed their minds and bought the unfinished boat back again, losing £300 in the process. Laurent Giles named the yacht *Peter Duck*, and it proved to be one of his most successful designs, with almost forty similar vessels built after Ransome's.

Apart from the trials and tribulations of building the new boat, the peace of their new home in central London was frequently destroyed by a noisy wireless and a howling baby in neighbouring flats. However, life was not all a matter of disturbance. They had a large work room in which Ransome could continue his writing and, still relishing a game of chess or billiards, he joined the Garrick Club. There he played chess against the playwright Terence Rattigan, and on one occasion he took part in a chess match between a team from Norfolk and Suffolk and one from Essex. *Cocky* was brought down from Coniston and he sailed on the River Thames from time to time. He visited Twickenham with the publisher Rupert Hart-Davis (who was to become his literary executor) and watched a thrilling Rugby match in which England narrowly defeated Scotland. For those who shared his interests, Ransome, with his white walrus moustache, twinkling eyes and hearty laugh, was good company. Few outside his immediate circle knew of his continuing poor health. For years he was never without a small suitcase which contained a bottle of milk, another of bismuth and a packet of biscuits. At regular intervals he took his bismuth in a small

glass of milk and followed this with a biscuit. He also had to be very careful never to eat anything which had been cooked in aluminium — something Evgenia was very particular about.

With the draft of *Great Northern?* finally finished in February 1946, he asked Wren Howard to read it, and was encouraged to go ahead. In July Ransome returned to Lewis to work on his revisions and prepare some sketches. By the end of the year the book was completed. As usual, Ransome was far from satisfied with his efforts and thought both beginning and end 'very bad'. Many of his readers, on the other hand, find the opening of the story to be one of his best.

The Swallows, Amazons and Ds have spent a fortnight cruising round the Hebrides with Captain Flint aboard a borrowed yacht called the *Sea Bear*. They sail into a sheltered cove just as a mist descends and blindly anchor in what they hope is the right place. Next morning they beach the Sea Bear so that they can scrub below her waterline before sailing back to the mainland. The four younger ones are allowed to explore while their elders are hard at work. Dick goes off alone as the others wander up the valley and unwittingly attract the attention of the local ghillies who suspect them of trying to drive the deer to another part of the island. Dick discovers 'nesting on the loch' a pair of birds which he believes to be great northern divers. His book tells him that these particular divers do not nest in Britain. When the *Sea Bear* arrives at the main island harbour to fill up with petrol, he takes the opportunity to call on a 'bird man' in order to be sure. The man turns out to be a professional egg-collector who not only confirms Dick's identification but wants to shoot the birds, take the eggs and claim the credit for the discovery. Captain Flint agrees to prolong the cruise for another day or two before returning the *Sea Bear* to her owner so that Dick can photograph the birds and thereby prove that they really have nested. In order to give Dick a fair chance of success, the egg collector and the Gaels have to be lured away from the loch where the birds are nesting, and the climax of the story is as satisfying as any in the series.

The Swallows and Amazons seem scarcely any older, though they have developed over the past five books. While Nancy masterminds their strategy, she still cannot resist turning a serious matter into a game. Once they have been captured by the Gaels, she remarks with adolescent disdain: 'That boy looks quite decent. Rather a waste really. We might have kidnapped him if we'd known and turned him into an ally. Barbecued billygoats! We could have kept him prisoner in the *Sea Bear*.' Ian, the 'young chieftain' to whom Nancy refers, and the surly dog-mudgeon are kilted Highlanders that the Hebridean setting allowed Ransome to introduce. The egg collector, with his 'protruding teeth and aquisitive nose', who wears a cap and plus-fours on board his yacht, is a creation of Myles North

Myles North's synopsis contained the essentials of the plot of *Great Northern?*, but Ransome ignored the rather far-fetched suggestion that Peter Duck and the red-haired Bill should turn up as crew aboard the egg-collector's yacht. North's suggestion had been that Captain Flint should take the children to the Hebrides aboard the *Wild Cat* — presumably he had not read *Missee Lee* in which that ship was burnt. Instead, Ransome modelled the *Sea Bear* on the *Teddy*, a 40-foot ex-pilot cutter in which Erling Tambs had made an epic voyage. Setting out from Norway with his bride aboard the *Teddy*, and without money or navigation instruments, Tambs began a cruise which ended three years later when the *Teddy* was wrecked off the coast of New Zealand. Ransome, who had been hugely impressed by Tambs' achievement, wrote an introduction to the first English edition of his book *The Cruise of the Teddy* in 1933.

Some readers have placed *Great Northern?* as a fantasy alongside *Peter Duck* and *Missee Lee*, although the story has little in common with those 'wild tales' and a great deal more with the 'realistic' stories. Ransome makes no mention of the time of the year or of a return to school, and this omission alone seems to provide support for their theory. In his synopsis North set the story in the middle of August and told Ransome that it was '...late, but not impossibly so. In fact, if the following points are brought out, I do not think that anyone could criticise: (a) That the eggs seem nearly hatching. (b) That they are very late. (c) That the birds must almost certainly have had a first brood in June, that went wrong, this second clutch being laid in July.' In this view he is supported by the ornithologist James Fisher in his second volume of *Bird Recognition*. Ransome thought that the laird's hos-

tility to trespassers should be based on his fear that they were disturbing the hinds shortly before they were due to drop their calves at the end of May, or in early June. This created a credibility problem which had not existed in North's plot, and which Ransome chose to ignore or felt he could do nothing about. 'Time. June would be the best. Why they are not at school, heaven only knows!!!!!'

Great Northern? carries a note which tells readers that 'Every effort has been made (short of falsifying the course of events) to prevent the inquisitive reader from learning the exact place where the *Sea Bear* was scrubbed and the Ship's Naturalist made his discovery.' Explorers should take the usual care not to intrude upon breeding birds and do nothing to harm the places where they live, but I have been assured that visitors in the breeding season are unlikely to come upon any nesting great northern divers. Around twenty pairs of black-throated divers nest on the freshwater lochs of the island and these are susceptible to disturbance by boats and anglers. Great northern divers have never been known to nest in the Western Isles, although in 1970 a pair and two fledglings were observed over a period of several weeks somewhere in Wester Ross on the mainland.

A little detective work is enough to reveal that the Head is Tiumpan Head and the harbour is Stornoway. Based on this information, Scrubbers' Cove and its neighbour ought to lie on the east side of Lewis, about ten miles north of Stornoway. The country to the north of Stornoway must be some of the wildest in Britain — a wilderness of lochs and rough moorland more than ten miles across between the roads which follow the coast. Yet while it is perfect country for the decoys and red herrings to lead their pursuers — and there are plenty of peat cuttings of the sort that Roger used to make his escape from the Gaels — the square-topped hill and distant mountains sound more like the southern end of the island.

When Roger reaches the top of the hill overlooking Scrubbers' Cove and discovers a circular grass-covered mound, Ransome presents the literary detective with something of a problem. Dorothea recognises the earthwork at once: 'It's a Pict-house. A real one. Prehistoric like the one they showed us on Skye.' Dorothea's grasp of history seems to let her down for once, and the next

(This page, top)
Uig Bay with its wide sandy beach was one of Ransome's favourite haunts.

(Left)
Ransome stayed at Uig Lodge which became the model for Dorothea's castle.

(Opposite page, top)
Uig Gorge.
(Malcolm Morrison)

(Lower left)
Uig Gorge drawing from Ransome's sketchbook. (Leeds U.)

(Lower right)
Unrealised sketches of the capture of the egg-collector.
(Abbot Hall)

moment she is wondering whether to have her next hero a prehistoric warrior, wearing skins and watching the Danish longships arrive. No less an authority than W. G. Collingwood asserts that the earliest Viking raids took place in the eighth century. School history books still speak of the 'Picts and Scots' at that period, although the word 'pict' is of much earlier origin and means 'painted one'.

Ian, Dorothea's 'young chieftain' uses the Pict-house as his private hiding-place. Ransome is careful to say that it is 'the grass-covered ruin that he [Ian] called the broch' — perhaps implying that the word is used loosely. There are plenty of examples of brochs to be found in the Western Isles and on Skye but these have stone walls in various stages of decay and are considerably larger. The Pict-house is certainly not a first-century broch.

It seems more likely that the Pict-house is a much older monument, and was a chamber burial place dating from 3-4,000 years BC. The chamber was frequently not central and was reached by means of a short narrow passage from outside. This certainly corresponds with Dick's drawing. The shallow bowl on top of the mound would have been formed when the roof of the chamber collapsed. Rather than speaking of a Pictish burial place, perhaps Ransome chose a more felicitous name in Pict-house.

Ransome carefully drew the 'queer low cottages' that Titty remembered were called 'black houses'. These were built as the crofter's universal response to the adverse climate. Doors and windows were kept to an absolute minimum and the walls were constructed of two drystone layers with earth filling the gap between. Rain ran down the roof and into the gap between the walls, thus ensuring that the earth remained moist and helping to keep the draughts out and the walls intact. The roof of straw thatch needed regular renewing if it was to keep out the elements. There are no inhabited black houses on Lewis these days as they have been replaced by modern bungalows. Away from the town of Stornoway, the island communities consist of a group of bungalows ranged alongside a narrow country road, each bungalow with its croft, or grazing land, for sheep. Most black houses quickly became ruins, with the notable exception of the one which was preserved as a museum at Arnol, complete with a peat fire burning to provide an authentic atmosphere.

The Clyde Cruising Club's Sailing Directions for the Outer Hebrides contains a number of small charts, none of which show an anchorage remotely like Scrubbers' Cove, though the Ordnance Survey map does indicate two small inlets called Port Bun a' Ghlinne in almost the right place, ten miles north-east of Stornoway. Beside the more northerly cove there is Gull Cliff, and rising from the top of the cliff, an admirable Pict-house Hill gives a wonderful view along the coast. Of course, there is no way of knowing if Ransome ever visited this delightful spot, but it has exactly the right feel about it. No doubt he mixed his usual geographical cocktail by adding some features of Uig Bay on the Atlantic coast, where he stayed on fishing trips. Uig Bay, with its wide sandy beaches and beautiful mountain scenery, is a captivating place and it is little wonder that, having discovered it, Ransome returned time and time again. He stayed with the Dobson family at Uig Lodge, which overlooks the bay and is instantly recognisable to readers as the Castle of the Gaels. Chief gamekeeper at the lodge was Roderick Mackenzie, and it was he who instructed Ransome in the use of Gaelic and later checked the story for errors. The pair became very friendly, and Mackenzie was probably given a small part in the story as Roderick the shepherd. Uig Gorge waterfall can be recognised from the drawing 'Portage', showing the folding boat on its way to the loch where the divers were nesting. There are no red deer in the part of Lewis where the story is set, although a few are to be found around Uig.

Great Northern? was published in August 1947 with an unusual error in one of the illustrations. In the drawing of the explorers on Pict-house Hill Peggy, instead of Titty, is shown sitting beside a rather tall Dorothea. This was easily remedied, but so rapidly were new printings appearing that it was not until the fourth edition that the books included the corrected drawing. Ransome's final illustration, showing Ian watching the *Sea Bear* sail out of sight, has been seen as a conscious farewell to the Swallows and Amazons. Yet the following year he wrote telling Wren Howard that he had '...at least two stories in the stocks — adventures that have their place in the series and ghosts of others waiting their turn'.

EPILOGUE

Arthur Ransome was sixty-three when *Great Northern?* was published, and he still had more than a dozen years of active life ahead of him. The summer and autumn of 1947 were taken up with sailing *Peter Duck* around his old haunts on the East Coast. Slowly he began to recognise the boat's good qualities, but his disgust with the designer over what he saw as careless mistakes inevitably effected his judgment. He was unable to find an anchor chain to fit *Peter Duck's* winch, and this and numerous other frustrations, which he chronicled in the log, prompted him to sell the boat in 1949. Two years later the Ransomes spent much of the summer looking for a suitable replacement. In September they were able to charter a 5-ton cruiser, designed and built by David Hillyard at his Littlehampton boatyard in Sussex. The fortnight's 'lazy carpet-slippered cruise' was so enjoyable that, when it was over, they visited Hillyard and ordered a similar vessel to be built for the following season.

For the next three summers the Ransomes sailed on the South Coast, first in a centre-cockpit sloop and finally in a similar hull but with the cockpit situated aft, which suited them better. In 1953 they took *Lottie Blossom* across the English Channel to Cherbourg, and repeated the voyage the following year. Ransome had not been out of sight of land since crossing the North Sea in 1936 and, for a man in poor health at the age of seventy, these were brave passages indeed, requiring both courage and good seamanship.

He ended his sailing career at that point at Evgenia's insistence and with some regret, but with the knowledge that he would now be free to concentrate on fishing. He still thought nothing of wading up to his chest in the fast-running River Leven, between Windermere and Morecambe Bay, in search of salmon. In the mid-1950s he caught his largest brown trout and sea trout, and in September 1960, at the age of 76, he landed his last fish — a 7lb salmon.

Meanwhile, in 1948, the Ransomes had bought Lowick Hall near the foot of Coniston Water. The property consisted of a large old house in need of repair and a nearby farm. It was only a matter of weeks before they realised that it was too much for them to take on, although they remained there for more than two years before putting it on the market and moving back to London. Here they found a flat in Hurlingham Court, Fulham, beside the River Thames. In the summer of 1955 they rented Ealinghearth Cottage, Haverthwaite, overlooking the Rusland Valley between Windermere and Coniston. The following year they were back at Haverthwaite, this time at Hill Top Cottage, and for a few years they spent the summers in the lake country and the winters in London.

As a writer, Ransome still had much to accomplish when he finally finished with the adventures of Nancy Blackett and her friends. Ever since his youth he had made a point of reading sea stories, and when Rupert Hart-Davis left Jonathan Cape to start his own publishing business and began to reprint cruising classics in the distinguished Mariner's Library series, Ransome took an interest in the undertaking. He bought some shares in the company and became its 'godfather and nanny'. The first title, published in 1948, was Joshua Slocum's 'lovable and simple-hearted book', *Sailing Alone Around the World*, which had long been one of Ransome's favourites. He wrote a special introduction to the book, as well as to four others, and was immensely helpful in compiling

(Opposite page)
Arthur Ransome

(This page, top)
Lowick Hall. The Ransomes made many internal improvements to this Norman Manorial Hall during their two year stay.
(Ted Alexander)

(Right)
Ransome convalescing at Pagham near Bognor Regis in 1969 aged 75.

the series which eventually ran to around fifty titles, including Ransome' own book, *Racundra's First Cruise*.

In 1959, thirty years after *Rod and Line*, Ransome published a second volume of fishing essays which he called *Mainly about Fishing*. The earlier volume is concerned with the joys of being a fisherman — joys which Ransome evokes so brilliantly that the book can be enjoyed even by those who have never held a rod. *Mainly About Fishing*, on the other hand, is for the dedicated fly-fisherman.

It was some ten years since he had begun to put together his *Autobiography*, a task which was never completed, although he worked at it from time to time until the early 60s. The manuscript required substantial reorganisation and editing by Rupert Hart-Davis, who had promised Ransome that he would see the book through the press. The difficulty was caused by Ransome's habit of starting with whatever chapter appealed and seemed easiest, leaving the most difficult chapters until last. *The Autobiography of Arthur Ransome* was eventually published after Evgenia's death in 1976, with a prologue and epilogue by Hart-Davis.

One of the reasons Ransome gave for writing the book was to acknowledge the debt he owed to his mentor, W. G. Collingwood. This favour was not granted to Collingwood's grandchildren, for there is no mention of the part they had played in the inspiration of *Swallows and Amazons*. Ransome's main problem seems to have been with Ernest Altounyan whose claims for his family had upset Ransome. If he was fearful for his reputation, he had no need. By the 1950s writing for children had become respectable — something for which he himself was partly responsible — and public recognition followed. In 1948 he received an honorary MA from Durham University, which disgusted him when he learned that Edith Sitwell was to get an honorary doctorate at the same ceremony. He did not have long to wait, however before receiving more appropriate rewards, for a couple of years later the University of Leeds gave him an honorary doctorate for his literary achievements, and in 1953 he was awarded a CBE.

The most memorable parts of Ransome's memoirs concern his youth. The holidays he spent at Nibthwaite are recalled with great clarity and affection:

> We used to catch minnows in the little cut where the Swainsons kept their boat, and we were taken perch-fishing, each of us watching a float of a different colour. This, of course, was very different from watching someone else catch fish. Then too, sometimes, when my father was fishing the lake for trout he would row his whole family up to Peel Island where we landed in the lovely little harbour at the south end (that some who have read my books as children may recognise borrowed for the sake of secrecy to improve an island on another lake). We spent the day as savages. My mother would settle down to make a sketch in water-colours. My father, forgetting to eat his sandwiches, would drift far along the lake-shores, casting his flies and coming back in the evening with trout in the bottom of the boat for Mrs Swainson to cook for next day's breakfast.

More than a third of the book is devoted to the seven years Ransome spent mostly in eastern Europe, for he had collected a wealth of material at the time he was planning to write a history of the Russian Revolution. The published version ends in 1932, although he wrote a rough draft for the years up to the Second World War which still exists among his archives at Abbot Hall Museum, Kendal. There is scarcely a reference to Arthur's courtship of Evgenia in his *Autobiography* and very little about his mother, who remained a source of financial support for a number of years and to whom he wrote at least once a week. The bitterness which he felt towards his first wife for so many years is evident in his writing. Although Ivy had died in 1939, only at the last did his feelings moderate.

On 1st December 1958 Ransome slipped on the front steps of the Cape offices in Bedford Square and fell. Although he appeared to suffer no more than a grazed knee, he was soon experiencing severe back pains and by the New Year was receiving treatment that at first paralysed him and then left him bed-ridden in often sleepless agony. A sound diagnosis eluded his doctors until, in July, he begged to be allowed to go home. As soon as he was stretchered out of hospital he began an astonishing recovery, but it was not to last. His strength had begun to diminish and, despite his devotion to her, he grew more querulous in the care of 'The Boss' (Evgenia) as her fluctuating moods and ill-temper spoke of the strain she was under. She took him off to Haverthwaite in the summer of 1960 and decided, against her better judgment, to buy the Hill Top cottage they had previously rented, despite its dilapidation. A year later Ransome wrote to Wren Howard from Haverthwaite as Penguin Books were preparing the first paperback edition of Swallows and Amazons:

> I have had another very bad tumble down from the steep hill outside my house, but am extremely lucky in that my spectacles, though wrecked, were not driven into my eyes. A further bit of good fortune was that after I had lain for some time in a puddle of gore, I came to and heard a car coming UP the hill (if it had been coming down nothing would have saved me...), lifted a Red Hand of Ulster and flapped it from road level, pouring with blood, and the car pulled up instantly, and from it on the run came a young woman, full of good sense, who pulled me round so that my head was no longer downhill, and explained that she was a qualified nurse and happened to be driving slowly because she once upon a time had two aunts who lived in this house...

Having had 'a bit of a shock', he told his publisher that he would be 'another two days before writing a considered report' on the Penguin cover design. Soon afterwards he wrote to tell Rupert Hart-Davis that he was feeling 'extremely lonely':

> The builders thunder upstairs and downstairs and fill the rooms with dust and rubble, besides WHUST-LING non-stop. Small hope of going fishing. Not that I really want to. What I do want is someone with whom to chatter. My best and oldest friends up here have fallen into the bad habit of dying...I can't walk with longer than six-inch strides!...I am more than ever persuaded that I ought to chuck any idea of autobiography. We'll talk of it again when I come back to town [the Ransomes kept their Fulham flat until 1963} but I don't want to have to contradict things said by other people who seem to me to have been trying to write my life for me.

Whatever bitter thoughts Ransome may have harboured towards her father, Ransome carefully preserved this drawing made by Titty when she was thirteen of a favourite doll.
(Leeds U.)

The death of Ernest Altounyan in 1962 revived one bitter resentment over what he saw as an attempt to reconstruct his life for him. With obsessive indignation, Ransome read in *The Times* obituary that the Altounyan children were the models for the Swallows, suggesting even that their father was due some credit for the books. He refused the *Manchester Guardian's* invitation to write on the subject; only his affection for Dora preventing him from making an inflammatory and scarcely honest statement of denial in the press. He omitted Altounyan altogether from his account of the genesis of *Swallows and Amazons* in his *Autobiography*, only grudgingly admitting that Altounyan's children 'had identified themselves (regardless of sex) with my characters' once the book was finished.

The letters from fans continued to pour in and Wren Howard had to carry some of the burden of replying:

> There are, perhaps, not real people in the sense that you are a real person and I am a real person, but

(Above)
Ransome's watercolour sketch of Baltic Port made during their stay in 1924. The schooner looks remarkably like the **Wild Cat** *in Peter Duck.*
(Leeds U)

(Right)
Ransome's watercolour painting of irises is one of the few to have survived.
(Leeds U.)

there is no doubt that people like them did exist. and still exist; Dr Ransome put his imagination to work on those people, and then produced the characters.

Over the years, Wren Howard contributed much to the success of the Swallows and Amazons books, and he continued to look after Ransome long after the last of the series was published. If anything, their correspondence increased following the publication of *Great Northern?* There are letters urging reprints, letters arguing over royalties and letters fuming over radio and television adaptations, although, surprisingly, Wren Howard does not seem to have urged Ransome to continue the series. They still addressed one another as 'Dear Ransome', and 'Dear Howard', although Wren Howard had sailed with Ransome aboard *Nancy Blackett* and they had worked together for over thirty years. What remains of their correspondence confirms that beneath all Ransome's bluster was an author painfully unsure of himself and forever at the mercy of his wife's unstinting criticism. Ransome had endured terrible troubles over *Winter Holiday* and without such a patient and long-suffering 'editor' it is probable that the series would have ended with *Peter Duck*. Several times Ransome was so late delivering the typescript for the Christmas market that it went straight to the printers, and Wren Howard only got to read it in proof — or even after it had been published!

By 1964, with their London flat gone, Arthur was confined to a wheel-chair on the upper floor of their remote lakeland home, where Evgenia was finding it increasingly difficult to manage. When she suffered two mild heart attacks in the autumn of 1965, she reluctantly accepted that, for the sake of the health of them both, Arthur needed the constant care of hospital nursing. For twenty months he lingered on, sometimes able to hold a conversation, often unaware of his surroundings. He died peacefully in Cheadle Royal Hospital near Manchester on 3rd June 1967.

In the closing words of his address at a Memorial Service held at St Martin's-in-the-Fields in London Sir Rupert Hart-Davis made the perfect summary of Arthur Ransome's contribution to English literature by saying... 'he is assured of exactly the kind of immortality he would have chosen — not the writing of learned theses on his work, nor critical assessments of his genius, but the voices of generation after generation of children, delightedly asking their parents: "Is it real?"'

A couple of years ago Ted Alexander came across a most moving note of confession among Ransome's papers in the Brotherton Collection at Leeds University, concerning what he had written about his matrimonial difficulties with his first wife, Ivy:

For my Literary Executor, poor chap.

It is unfair to tell any such story from one side only...I have always felt that if she had married a man of her own kind, an actor perhaps, or a politician, as whose wife she would have had the opportunity of furthering his career by public appearances, she would have been better and happier. Or, if she had been an actress she might have found an outlet for just those gifts that she felt were being wasted. In any case, I am to blame for not having the courage to run away before it was too late. And I deserved some sort of punishment for my light-minded and idiotic habit of gaily proposing to every young woman I met and of writing a love letter (to someone or other, real or imaginary) after breakfast as a way of beginning the day's work.

Also I do not think I have made it clear that she was extraordinarily attractive to all men, including myself. My very efforts to escape must have seemed to her (as indeed she said) wilful and wrong-headed. It was as if she felt she had to cure me from being myself. How could I not perceive that all the others envied me for being married to her?

Finally, I should not have agreed to leave my library in her keeping, but as Lascelles said, should have removed it and myself once and for all so that there could be no pretence that I was coming back.

BIBLIOGRAPHY

Books by Arthur Ransome

The Desert Island (1892), The Arthur Ransome Society's Journal, 1990.
The ABC of Physical Culture , Henry Drane, 1904
The Souls of the Streets, Brown Langham, 1904.
The Stone Lady, Brown, Langham, 1905.
The Things in our Garden, Anthony Treherne, 1906.
Pond and Stream, Anthony Treherne, 1906.
Things in Season, Anthony Treherne, 1906.
Highways and Byways in Fairyland, Alston Rivers, 1907.
Bohemia in London, Chapman & Hall, 1907.
A History of Storytelling, TC & EC Jack, 1909.
The Book of Friendship, TC & EC Jack, 1909.
Edgar Allan Poe, Martin Secker, 1910.
The Book of Love, TC & EC Jack, 1911.
The Hoofmarks of the Faun, Martin Secker, 1911.
Oscar Wilde, Martin Secker, 1912.
Portraits and Speculations, Macmillan, 1913.
The Elixir of Life, Methuen, 1915.
Old Peter's Russian Tales, TC & EC Jack, 1916.
Aladdin and his Wonderful Lamp, Nisbet, 1919.
Six Weeks in Russia in 1919, George Allen & Unwin, 1921.
The Soldier and Death, JG Wilson, 1920.
The Crisis in Russia, George Allen & Unwin, 1921.
Racundra's First Cruise, George Allen & Unwin, 1923.
The Chinese Puzzle, George Allen & Unwin, 1927
Rod and Line, Cape, 1929.
Swallows and Amazons, Cape 1930.
Swallowdale, Cape 1931.
Peter Duck, Cape 1932.
Winter Holiday, Cape 1933.
Coot Club, Cape 1934.
Pigeon Post, Cape 1936.
We Didn't Mean to Go to Sea, Cape, 1937.
Secret Water, Cape, 1939.
The Big Six, Cape, 1940
Missee Lee, Cape, 1941.
The Picts and the Martyrs, Cape, 1943.
Great Northern?, Cape, 1947.
Mainly About Fishing, A&C Black, 1959.
Autobiography, Edited and with an introduction by Rupert Hart-Davis, Cape, 1976.
Coots in the North, Cape, 1988.
Signalling from Mars, a selection of letters edited and introduced by Hugh Brogan, Cape, 1997.

Taqui Altounyan, *In Aleppo Once*, John Murray, 1969.
Hugh Brogan, *The Life of Arthur Ransome*, Cape, 1984.
WG Collingwood, *The Lake Counties*, Dent 1902.
GC Davies, *The Swan and her Crew*, Warne 1876.
Christina Hardyment, *Arthur Ransome and Captain Flint's Trunk*, Cape, 1984.
Eric Holland, *Coniston Copper*, Cicerone Press, 1986.
Michael Howard, *Jonathan Cape, Publisher*, Cape, 1971.
Katharine Hull and Pamela Whitlock, *The Far-Distant Oxus*, Cape 1937.
Peter Hunt, *Approaching Arthur Ransome*, Cape, 1992.
Claire Kendall-Price, *In the Footsteps of the Swallows and Amazons*, Wild Cat publishing, 1993.
Lola Kinel, *Under Five Eagles*, 1938.
EF Knight, *The Cruise of the Falcon*, Sampson Low, 1884
EF Knight, *The Cruise of the Alerte*, 1890.
Aleko Lilius, *I Sailed with Chinese Pirates*, JW Arrowsmith, 1930.
Robert Bruce Lockhart, *Memoirs of a British Agent*, Putnam, 1932.
Pauline Marshall, *Where it all Began*, 1991.
Graham Ritchie and Mary Harman, *Exploring Scotland's Heritage*, HMSO, 1985.
William Rollinson, *The Lake District Life and Traditions*, Weidenfeld & Nicolson, 1996.
Hugh Shelley, *Arthur Ransome*, Bodley Head 1960.
Erling Tambs, *The Cruise of the Teddy*, Newnes, 1933.
Roger Wardale, *Arthur Ransome's East Anglia*, Poppyland Publishing, 1988.
Roger Wardale, *Nancy Blackett: Under Sail with Arthur Ransome*, Cape 1991.
Roger Wardale, *In Search of Swallows and Amazons*, Sigma Leisure, 1996.

The Clyde Cruising Club's sailing Directions for The Outer Hebrides.
The Cruising Association Handbook, 1928.
The Outer Hebrides Handbook and Guide, Kittywake Press, 1995
Norfolk Broads Holidays Afloat, Blakes (Norfolk Broads Holidays) Ltd, 1947.

INDEX